BRISTOL & BATH
RAILWAYS

Colin Maggs

THE AGE OF STEAM

COUNTRYSIDE BOOKS

NEWBURY BERKSHIRE

First published 2011
© Colin Maggs 2011

COUNTRYSIDE BOOKS
3 Catherine Road
Newbury, Berkshire

To view our complete range of books,
please visit us at
www.countrysidebooks.co.uk

ISBN 978 1 84674 204 0

Designed by Peter Davies, Nautilus Design
Produced through MRM Associates Ltd., Reading
Typeset by CJWT Solutions, St Helens
Printed by Information Press, Oxford

Contents

Acknowledgements 4

Abbreviations 4

Chapter 1   **The Start of the Steam Age** 5

Chapter 2   **The Network Expands from Bristol** 18

Chapter 3   **Improvements for Bath** 27

Chapter 4   **Running the Railways** 32

Chapter 5   **Bristol's Locomotives** 57

Chapter 6   **Goods in Transit – Coal, Bananas and Wagons of Wind** 62

Chapter 7   **Stations and Signals** 76

Chapter 8   **Fresh Milk and Strawberries** 83

Chapter 9   **Race Days and Football Specials** 86

Chapter 10   **Time for a Good Book** 89

Chapter 11   **Railways at War** 92

Chapter 12   **Tragedy on the Line** 105

Chapter 13   **The Glories of the Past** 114

Chapter 14   **Steam Today** 122

Bibliography 124

Appendix: Bristol and Bath Railway Chronology 125

Index 126

Acknowledgements

Many thanks are due to Colin Roberts for checking the manuscript.

Abbreviations

AGR	Avon & Gloucestershire Railway
B&E	Bristol & Exeter Railway
BGR	Bristol & Gloucestershire Railway
BHR	Bristol Harbour Railway
BNSR	Bristol & North Somerset Railway
BPRP	Bristol Port Railway & Pier
BSWUR	Bristol & South Wales Union Railway
CER	Clifton Extension Railway
GWR	Great Western Railway
LMS	London, Midland & Scottish Railway
LNER	London & North Eastern Railway
MR	Midland Railway
PBA	Port of Bristol Authority
S&D	Somerset & Dorset (later 'Joint') Railway

The Start of the Steam Age

It is often said that the north-east of England is 'the cradle of the railways', but the Bath and Bristol area can also lay claim to a share in this title and it all dates back to the time, early in the 18th century, when Bath was expanding rapidly.

As the spa town grew, large blocks of stone weighing four tons or more that were quarried on the hills to the south needed to be transported easily and cheaply to the building sites 500 ft below and 1½ miles distant. The quarry owner believed that his enterprise could be made even more profitable by using barges to take stone downstream to Bristol for use there and also for export. But how could the stone be carried easily and cheaply down to the river?

The answer was a 'railway'. Timber rails were set on a gradient of 1 in 10, which meant that loaded vehicles could descend by gravity, horses only being required for shunting and drawing empty wagons uphill. The line opened in 1731, lowering the price of stone by a quarter. Rails were later laid on the north side of the River Avon and wagons carried across on barges – the train ferry had been invented!

The whole line fell out of use in the late 1760s, but the idea was not forgotten and 30 years later when the Kennet and Avon Canal was cut, similar double-acting inclines were built linking various quarries with the waterway.

Almost concurrently the Somerset Coal Canal was cut to form a branch from the Kennet and Avon and serve collieries in the Cam Valley, south of Bath. This branch canal was made from Midford to Radstock, but as there was a considerable difference between the two levels, a mile-long railway provided a link. In the event, this Radstock arm saw little use due to the cost of transporting goods, so in 1814 it was decided to abandon the Radstock reach and extend the railway to Radstock. Teams of three horses hauled trains of eight to nine

Ralph Allen's railway, with his mansion Prior Park in the background. Two loaded stone wagons are descending by gravity, controlled by a brakesman at the rear. (Author's collection)

wagons, each holding 27 hundredweights of coal. The line was single with passing loops. On the occasions when trains met head-on, the two drivers fought for precedence. On high days and holidays the wagons were brushed out and used for passenger traffic to Radstock, with planks laid across for seating. In due course, this interesting line was taken over by the Somerset & Dorset Railway when it built its extension to Bath.

At this time William Ashman, engineer to the Clandown Colliery, designed a lightweight steam locomotive. It began work in August 1827, but unfortunately proved too heavy for the frail track and had to be withdrawn.

A coalfield north of Bristol was served by the Bristol & Gloucestershire Railway (BGR). The northern section of the route from Coalpit Heath to Mangotsfield was to be shared with the Avon & Gloucestershire Railway (AGR), the latter running down to the Avon opposite Keynsham. This northern section opened in July 1832, together with the AGR. Both lines were horse-worked, fortunately the gradient favouring the load. The BGR opened to Bristol on 6 August 1835 and was the city's first railway.

The cutting approaching the Avon & Gloucestershire's
Willsbridge Tunnel c.1900. (Author's collection)

Prior to opening, a Bond & Winwood-designed locomotive had been tried, but exploded, sending parts flying up to 300 yards away after a modification had been made to increase its speed in order that it could make two trips, instead of one, daily. Its steam was generated in tubes rather than in a boiler.

FROM HORSE POWER TO STEAM POWER

Although the horse-worked BGR was successful, an extension to Gloucester was called for and, on 9 September 1839, Isambard Kingdom Brunel was appointed engineer to another company, the Bristol & Gloucester Railway. Although initially he agreed to use the existing standard gauge, to reduce costs, it was deemed expedient to share the northern part of the line with the broad gauge Cheltenham & Great Western Union Railway. Thus it was decided that the Bristol & Gloucester Railway should convert to broad gauge, though Staple Hill Tunnel and the bridges were never full broad gauge width. Staple Hill Tunnel was originally only 12 ft wide, but was widened to 26 ft by the Bristol & Gloucester. Because of its original single line construction, the two ventilating shafts which can still be seen today are over the site of the Down line. Care of

A broad gauge train crosses the viaduct west of Bath's GWR station c.1840. River traffic is still in evidence at the Broad Quay in the foreground. (Author's collection)

Water Carriage.

The Kennet and Avon Canal affords a direct Communication with London; and Goods are in general conveyed thither in five or six days from the following Warehouses:

A. J. DREWE's (late Betts and Drewe) Fly-Boats, daily, to and from Steel-yard Wharf, Thames street, London; and Darlington Wharf, near Sydney wharf, Bath, in five days regularly.

EUCLID SHAW and Co.'s Fly Boats, from Bull Wharf, Upper Thames street, London; to Sydney Wharf, Bath, in five days; and Bull Wharf, Redcliffe street, Bristol, in six days.

C. and R. PARKER' sFly-Boats, to and from Redcliff Back, Bristol, and Dorchester street, Bath, every day; and deliver goods at each place every morning; and to Marlborough, Bradford, Trowbridge, Devizes, Salisbury, Andover, &c., three times a week.

The *City of Bath*, Steam-Boat, for the conveyance of Passengers and Goods to and from Bristol; leaves the Old Bridge, Bath, every morning, (except Sunday) at 8, and returns the same evening.

Details of waterway communication with London. (Bath Directory, 1833)

the environment was considered: the earthworks were neatly covered with turf 'well beat and pressed into place' while £60 was paid to John Nelson for planting shrubs and trees at five of the company's stations.

Railway construction was fraught with danger and in November 1843 the Bristol Infirmary made a special application to the Bristol & Gloucester Railway as 13 'expensive casualties' had been sent there in the last twelve months. In response the railway added £20 to its normal subscription to the hospital of five guineas.

The Bristol & Gloucester's general superintendent was Wyndham Hardy, a contemporary, at Rugby School, of Thomas Hughes, author of *Tom Brown's Schooldays*. At that time, it was very unusual for a classical scholar to take up engineering.

Meanwhile, another group of Bristolians had been setting up the Great Western Railway (GWR) to link the city with London – the third main line that served Bristol was the broad gauge Bristol & Exeter Railway (B&E) which would continue the GWR westwards. A railway could speed goods between the cities in four hours instead of three days by road, or three weeks or more by canal. One Bath draper complained that fashion changed while his goods were

Midland Railway barges at Avonside Wharf, Bristol, June 1898. The nearest vessels are No 8 and No 6. This wharf was formerly the terminus of the Bristol & Gloucestershire Railway. In the background a GWR signal box is perched on a gantry. (Author's collection)

in transit, while a Bristol wine merchant stated that his beer and spirits were abstracted en route and replaced with water. By providing a speedier journey, the railway would address these problems including reducing the chance of theft.

One problem the GWR encountered was that as both Bath and Bristol stations were near river crossings, each had to be built at first-storey level to enable the adjacent bridges to offer sufficient height to allow waterway traffic safe passage beneath. The railway being on a viaduct proved useful in times of flood, as several adjacent householders were able to escape from their homes by way of the roof and the railway.

Brunel designed his Bristol terminus at Temple Meads to look like a Tudor mansion, the Elizabethan style also being used for the station at Bath and many of the intermediate bridges, tunnels and stations. Arguably the most impressive part of Brunel's Temple Meads station is the timber cantilever roof with a span of 72 ft. Unfortunately its supporting pillars were so close to the platform edge that there was too little clearance when coach doors were opened.

At the station itself, luggage was treated better than passengers. The former was carried between the floors by hydraulic lifts, but passengers had to use the stairs.

The site at Bath was between two bridges only 700 ft apart and in the space was squeezed a passenger station, engine shed and goods depot – the latter set at right angles to the main line and its access by wagon turntable. The passenger station was within a 40-ft span train shed and, as at Bristol, the columns were set too close to the platform edge. Here, each platform was served by two hydraulic lifts: one for passengers and the other for goods.

The station was approached by arches and in order to maximise revenue, these were let. To the east, in 1854, three arches were converted into a school, with a further arch and adjoining land providing a dry playground with flower borders. West of the station one arch formed a police station, another a mortuary, while a tea and coffee stall was set up beneath a road arch.

Construction of the GWR line between the two cities was far from

The east end of Temple Meads station in the 1860s, with the Bristol & Exeter timber-built terminus on the far left, and the B&E offices, centre. Notice the turntable for coaches and wagons and also the mixed gauge track. (Author's collection)

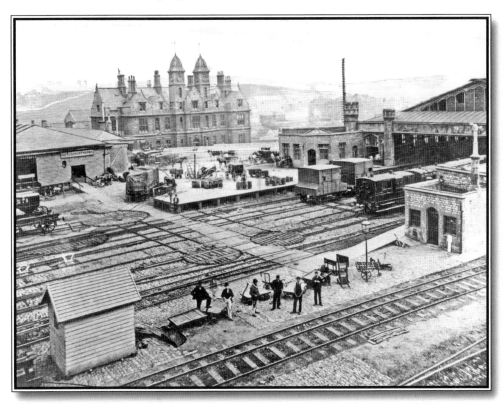

The GWR station at Bath c.1845. Notice that the columns supporting the train shed are very close to the platform edge – disembarking passengers are likely to bump into them. (J.C. Bourne)

straightforward. Five tunnels were required east of Bristol, plus one at Saltford and two at Twerton.

Navvies earned between four and eight shillings a day – very good pay compared with an agricultural worker's wage of nine to twelve shillings a week. One disadvantage of being well-paid was that the labourers had plenty of money to spend on quenching their thirst and this led to bad behaviour. Local residents subscribed to pay for chaplains to minister to their spiritual needs and hold special Sunday services. On 23 April 1838 near St Anne's Park, troops had to be called in when 300 navvies, most of whom had been born in Gloucestershire, attacked with spades, pickaxes and crowbars a similar number from Devonshire and West Somerset.

Only a few injuries to the navvies building this line are recorded in the local newspapers. On 20 June 1838, while cutting Twerton Tunnel, the plank on which four workmen were standing snapped; one man had to have his leg amputated, another had a broken leg, the third a severe spinal injury and the fourth a bruised and lacerated scalp. All were taken to the Bath United Hospital

Widcombe Infants' School in Bath, 1855, set below the railway viaduct.
(Author's collection)

and four days after admission the newspaper reported: 'The unfortunate sufferers are doing well.'

In November of the same year, a cutting slipped near Bristol, killing one navvy and seriously injuring three others who were taken to Bristol Infirmary. A few months later, brickwork in Bristol No 3 Tunnel collapsed, killing three men and injuring nine others.

The railway's completion meant that the navvies had to seek new work but not all were successful. On 6 January 1841 John Edwards, aged 32, died at Bath 'from want of necessities of life'. He had been unemployed for five weeks, ill for four days and he, his wife and 18 month old child were in a state of 'the most deplorable wretchedness'. The inquest found that the cold weather and lack of nourishment caused his death.

As the land required for Twerton Viaduct required the removal of several cottages, the landowner was paid £1,000 to demolish them. They were rebuilt as an integral part of the viaduct. The new dwellings had two rooms, each with a fireplace. The flue ran horizontally to a chimney designed as a buttress outside the southern wall. These houses soon fell out of use, probably due to the difficulty of getting the smoke to go out of the chimney – certainly vibration and dampness were not a problem.

The railway passed through Twerton vicarage garden and as the line was so close to the house, a new vicarage was built nearer the church. Unfortunately, before the incumbent could move into the new vicarage, navvies cut through the drains, thereby causing an outbreak of cholera that resulted in the death of the then vicar's son. A later occupant of the new vicarage was George Earle Buckle, who was born there on 10 June 1854: he became editor of *The Times* newspaper.

The bridge immediately west of Bath station was very much on the skew and said to be the most oblique bridge ever built of wood. Although the width of the river at that point was 80 ft, the space traversed by the railway was 164 ft. As the normal ironwork would have taken a long time to prepare, due to a national shortage of the metal, Brunel had decided he would construct it of timber. It

The GWR station at Bath viewed from Beechen Cliff c.1841.
Lower centre is the passenger station, while to the left, by the laminated
timber bridge, the goods station is set at right angles to the main line.
To the right, an Up express is crossing St James' Bridge.
(Author's collection)

was the only laminated timber bridge he built. Each rib was made from five layers of timber imported from Lithuania, bent by steam to the desired curvature and then held together by bolts and iron straps. The cornice and parapets were also of timber. To prevent rot, the wood was 'kyanised', that is, immersed in a solution of corrosive sublimate. This process became outdated when creosote was made available. Laminated timber arches usually had a life of less than 25 years because they were flexible and flexing caused the laminations to separate and thus allow water to enter and cause decay. This bridge, however, enjoyed a life of 38 years.

The erection of the coffer dam for the central pier and the actual construction of the bridge was a free public entertainment in the humdrum lives of many Bathonians. The *Bath & Cheltenham Gazette* of 17 September 1839 reported: 'Hundreds of our fellow-citizens of all classes daily visit the locality to witness the interesting and novel operations of the workmen.'

The *Bath & Cheltenham Gazette* also recorded the progress of the first train from Bristol to arrive at Bath:

> At about twenty minutes to nine the sounding of a bell announced the approach of the 'monster' with his screaming note and tribe of vehicles. The Fire Ball was decorated with small flags, and as it passed along the line was greeted with the most enthusiastic cheering of the spectators and workmen, the passengers responding by a waving of hats and handkerchiefs from the windows of the train. On reaching its destination the shouting was prodigiously increased. Each of the six carriages was filled by most respectable parties, who were quickly disembogued and the engine replenished with water. The belfry of the Abbey church contributed its quota to the hilarity of the day, and a few of the principal shops were partially closed. The first trip was performed in the space of 30 minutes; a period perhaps longer than some might have anticipated, but easily accounted for, on the ground that the full power of the engines not being tested, in consequence of the recent erection of a great portion of the works, and the fear of their being shaken by too great a speed.
>
> If, in the morning, Bristol sent forth its thousands to witness the opening of the line from Bristol to Bath, in the evening it sent forth its tens of thousands. The scene up the Bath road, on Pile Hill [modern spelling is 'Pylle Hill'], and every spot along both sides of the line, as far as we could catch a glimpse, up to the entrance of No. 1 tunnel, was nearly one mass of human beings, who 'one and all' expressed their hearty satisfaction by continued cheering and waving of handkerchiefs as the different trains passed, demonstrations which were enthusiastically responded to by the passengers; and all seemed gratified at the opening of a means of conveyance that has brought two of the principal cities in the country within a few minutes' ride of each other.

Due to the extensive works required for the cutting of Box Tunnel, the Chippenham to Bath section of the Bristol to London line was the last to be completed. The GWR usually offered landowners a fair price for their property. Just east of Bath station, the formation for the new railway was required to pass under Bathwick Terrace. This meant that most of it needed to be pulled down and rebuilt. The company offered Mr Mackay, owner of three houses in the terrace, £2,700. Dissatisfied with this sum he pressed for £3,200. The jury's verdict at arbitration was £2,650!

For the convenience of workmen going to and from their hutments at Bathford, the contractors had erected a temporary wooden bridge across the Avon. Immediately east of Bath station, St James' Bridge was being constructed. Its abutments had been built, massive piles driven deep into the river bed and strong centrings fixed, so all was ready for masons to commence making the arch. On 16 January 1841 a violent flood hurled the temporary bridge from Bathford against the centrings of St James' Bridge with such a terrific impact that they were swept away. A huge mass of woodwork then was carried down the river, some lodging against the skew bridge west of Bath station. The rest formed a partial dam at the Old Bridge, where the debris was secured by ropes and chains. A large quantity of tools belonging to the artisans at work on St James' Bridge was also lost, though the loss would have been greater had not work been temporarily suspended because of the frost. This episode cost the contractor £1,000.

A quieter tale of pathos was enacted on 14 March 1845, when John Jonathan, aged about 50, was travelling on the 10.10 am third class train from Bristol to Bath. Being so soon after the passing of Gladstone's Regulation of Railways Act of 9 August 1844, he was probably totally unaware that a closed third class coach had to be made available on the train in such cold conditions, so travelled in an open vehicle. On arrival at Bath he was frozen so stiff that he could not get out of the coach without the assistance of a porter. After the train's departure, the porter carried him downstairs to street level and, as John had expressed a desire for a drink, asked one of the urchins who frequented the station to take him to a nearby tavern. However, he collapsed in the street and died before medical assistance arrived.

At the inquest Mrs Jonathan revealed that their finances were insufficient to permit both to travel by train, so as he suffered from poor health, he rode, while she walked. In an effort to keep warm he was wearing two pairs of trousers, two waistcoats, two body coats and a woollen scarf. The inquest jury brought in the verdict: 'That the deceased died by the visitation of God, but that his death was accelerated by the inclemency of the weather to which he was exposed in a third class carriage of the Great Western Railway Company, the weather being unusually severe for March.'

The coming of the railways changed life in many ways. Apart from ousting coachmen, guards, ostlers, innkeepers, coach makers, harness makers, farriers, horse food growers and corn merchants from their prominence in a horse-drawn economy, the effects of new railways were wide-ranging as so many tradesmen were partly or wholly dependent on coach traffic. Each horse cost about £2 a week to feed. Hounslow had 2,500 horses which meant that at least £5,000 circulated in the town each week; *The Times* of 4 April 1839 said that the 70 coaches which had recently passed through Hounslow daily had been reduced to only nine or ten, with dire consequences for the traditional trades. Figures for the Bristol/Bath area would have been similar. Inns in towns usually survived by developing other trade, but isolated country inns suffered.

Stagecoach travel was fraught with danger and probably had a higher death and injury rate than any other previous or subsequent method of land travel. Drawn by fickle beasts, a coach had a high centre of gravity and could easily be upset by a pile of stones, an axle or pole breaking, harness snapping, or a wheel coming off. Since the 1830s the writing had been on the wall as coaches had had to contend with competition from steam-powered ships taking travellers around the coast. Ships paid no mileage duty, so the fare for the best cabin was half the duty alone for the same distance by coach. Coaches were licensed for a certain number of passengers and the mileage duty was payable on that number, whether or not the seats were actually occupied: now the railways only paid duty on the actual numbers carried and at a lower rate.

The Post Office guards that had travelled on Royal Mail stagecoaches were mainly unaffected as they simply changed to the railway at much the same salary. There is no record of coachmen finding work on the railway, but a considerable number were employed on the horse-drawn buses running feeder services to railway stations.

W. Pennell, the Poor Law Commissioner for the Midlands, said in 1842: 'The rail roads have driven the coaches off the roads, running at right angles with them, as well as parallel; and persons travelling short journeys, or those taking long journeys from and to places in planes lying at right angles with the rail roads are deprived of those facilities which they formerly had.' Thus stagecoach proprietors missed an opportunity that would later be filled by omnibus operators.

2

THE NETWORK EXPANDS FROM BRISTOL

OUT TO AVONMOUTH

On 10 November 1851 the winding River Avon's inadequacy in coping with the increasing size of vessels had been strikingly revealed when the bows of the 3,000-ton paddle steamer *Demerara*, built at Bristol and being towed to Glasgow for her engines to be fitted, struck a bank. She swung round, her stern hit the other bank and the ebbing tide caused her back to break. It was becoming obvious that facilities must be constructed nearer the sea and in order to avoid a repetition of this problem, ports were developed at Avonmouth and Portishead.

Initially Avonmouth was served by the Bristol Port Railway & Pier Company (BPRP), an independent line which started at Hotwells, below the Clifton Suspension Bridge. Because it was unconnected with other railway systems, it was principally a passenger line carrying workmen and holidaymakers. A leisure complex was set up at Avonmouth and proved enormously popular on bank holidays, attracting literally thousands of Bristolians. There was also a rifle range and on 16 February 1878 a Clifton College sixth-former, returning on the train from practice, accidentally discharged his rifle in the compartment, killing a master.

The fact that the BPRP was not linked to the rest of the railway system caused problems when a locomotive was under repair and a replacement had to be hired from the Midland Railway (MR). Of necessity it had to be conveyed along public roads on a horse-drawn lorry. On one such occasion the lorry

BPRP locomotive No 1, believed to have been built by the St Helen's Railway in 1856. (Author's collection)

sank into a soft patch of Perry Road and required no fewer than 60 horses to extricate it.

To enable Avonmouth to develop as a port, a rail link with the national system was essential. This was by the Clifton Extension Railway (CER) which ran from just north of Stapleton Road station to Sneyd Park Junction on the BPRP, near Sea Mills.

This line required a 1,768-yd-long tunnel to be bored below Clifton Downs. It was excavated with the aid of a diamond-boring machine invented by Major Beaumont, MP. Cutting facets of black diamond were fixed round the end of a steel tube to form an auger and the tube was revolved rapidly by compressed air. Water forced through the tube washed away grit and kept the tube cool. A blasting charge was then inserted into the hole made. Noise from the blasting made people reluctant to rent houses above the tunnel owned by the company. A tenant in one of the company's houses in Hampton Park was so disturbed that he was forced to leave and the CER paid him £30 compensation for removal expenses.

Although the CER was opened to freight traffic on 24 February 1877 – the day Avonmouth Dock station opened – the Board of Trade inspector would not

A 517 class 0-4-2T at Hotwells heads a train to Avonmouth in 1898.
The station is in a cramped position between the side of the gorge,
left, and the river, right. (Author's collection)

permit the line to be used for passenger traffic owing to a defect in the track and signalling at Sneyd Park Junction. Eventually matters were corrected and a passenger service began on 1 September 1885.

Clifton Down Tunnel rises on a gradient of 1 in 64 towards Clifton Down station. In steam days smoke tended to hang towards the Clifton Down portal and because their view was obscured, drivers could come upon the station before they were aware of it and thus over-run the platform. To overcome this problem, in 1924 a clapper and gong operated by the wheels of a passing train was installed near the exit to sound an audible warning.

In 1950, to improve ventilation provided by the two existing shafts, a horizontal tunnel leading to the face of the gorge was reopened. Originally it had been used as a stable for ponies employed in the tunnel's construction. A further interesting feature was a gangers' cabin hewn out of the side of the tunnel, approximately midway.

The eastern portal of the 1,768-yd-long Clifton Down Tunnel, May 1954.
Notice the house above. (Dr A.J.G. Dickens)

The BPRP experienced financial difficulties and was taken over jointly by the GWR and MR. The GWR underestimated the engine power necessary to work the line and the very first train stalled on the incline up to Horseshoe Point and required an assistant engine to come to the rescue. The *Bristol Times & Mirror* reported: 'We are informed that the exclamations of the most forcible character rang out on the morning air in lusty chorus from the 468 working men passengers who were subject to this delay.' Until the opening of the Severn Road Bridge in 1966, in addition to the normal traffic on the CER, 'Monkey Specials' were run from South Wales to Clifton Down station carrying visitors to the zoo. In due course, the line from Hotwells to Sneyd Park Junction was closed and made into the Portway, now the A4.

Around 1900 the stationmaster at Sea Mills diversified. In addition to his railway duties, he kept poultry, pigs and a cow and used his pony and trap to collect swill from Avonmouth Docks. He sold eggs to passengers and provided the GWR Superintendent at Bristol with butter and new-laid eggs. Another

character was 'Mad Jack', a driver who enjoyed scaring dockers half to death by rushing through the tunnels into the terminus at Hotwells. Once, he misjudged his braking power and crashed into the buffers.

BRINGING CARDIFF CLOSER

As the crow flies, Bristol is only 25 miles from Cardiff, but 150 years ago the rail distance via Gloucester was 93 miles. An improvement was called for. A sort of answer was the Bristol & South Wales Union Railway (BSWUR) which

The ceremonial opening of New Passage Pier, 25 August 1863. Trains ran to the far end of the pier. (Courtesy Illustrated London News)

John Aird used some 25 locomotives on his contract for building the Royal Edward Dock, Avonmouth. (J. Walford collection)

ran from South Wales Junction, half a mile east of Temple Meads, to New Passage Pier where a ferry crossed two miles of water to Portskewett Pier, also rail served.

The resident engineer for this work was Charles Richardson, who was to become chief engineer to the Severn Tunnel project (and also designed the sprung cricket bat handle).

Rowland Brotherhood of Chippenham was the contractor responsible for building the BSWUR and required locomotives to shift spoil from excavations to embankments. As it was difficult to move a railway locomotive along ordinary roads, Rowland's son, Peter, designed an engine capable of travelling on road or railway. In 1862, one of these 11-ton machines travelled by road from Chippenham to Patchway at an average speed of 6 mph.

Legend has it that on one rough crossing between the two piers, a nervous lady asked a sailor, 'Do ships often sink on this passage?' She was given the reply, 'Only once, madam, only once.'

TO PORTISHEAD AND CANON'S MARSH

The Bristol & Portishead Pier & Railway, a rival to the BPRP, ran from a junction with the B&E at Bedminster to a terminus and pier at Portishead. From there steamer services were operated by the railway to Cardiff and Newport, while trips to Ilfracombe were worked in the summer. The line was quite scenic, especially in the region of Clifton Bridge station. The delightfully-named Nightingale Valley Halt opened on 9 July 1928 for the benefit of trippers, but failed to receive the expected patronage and so closed on 12 September 1932.

Leading from the Portishead branch was the goods-only Bristol Harbour Railway (BHR) which served the harbour complex and rejoined the main line at Temple Meads. Its construction required the demolition of St Mary Redcliffe's

A 481 class 2-4-0 at Clifton Bridge heads an Up train in the 1890s.
(Author's collection)

vicarage and the cutting of a tunnel through a burial ground, involving the expense of removal and re-interment of corpses. The line also had a long viaduct, a tunnel and three bridges, the most interesting of which was an opening bascule bridge over Bathurst Basin – a lifting bridge worked by a counterpoise. Designed by Charles Richardson, it was powered by a horizontal steam engine.

As the BHR only served the Avon's south bank, the GWR built an extension from Ashton Junction to Canon's Marsh. Its most interesting engineering feature was Ashton Swing Bridge. As a road bridge was also required at this point, it was built with a double deck: the upper carrying a road and the lower a railway. The swing span, 202 ft in length, weighed 1,000 tons and was turned by hydraulic power. The two three-throw reversible engines working the bridge were situated in a control cabin set above the roadway.

To prevent a train falling into the water when the bridge was open for river

*Normally passenger trains were not seen on the Bristol Harbour Railway, but on
28 April 1957 the Railway Correspondence & Travel Society ran a special train
from Waterloo: Ivatt class 2 2-6-2T Nos 41202 and 41203 head the eight
coaches near Smeaton Road. (D. Priddy/Colin Roberts collection)*

The double-deck Ashton Swing Bridge. (Author's collection)

traffic, the bridge was interlocked with the GWR signal boxes on each side, making it impossible for railway signals to be cleared for the movement of a train unless the swing span was firmly secured. For safety, only one vessel was allowed to pass the bridge at a time. To control shipping movements, two cones were used. A north cone, point upwards, was lowered to permit a ship to move downstream, or a south cone lowered to allow a ship to move upstream.

NORTH SOMERSET

Although Radstock and its coalfield was served by the Somerset Coal Canal tramway, and from 1854 by a GWR branch from Frome, a direct line from Bristol was needed. This was the Bristol & North Somerset Railway (BNSR).

Construction started in 1863, but soon ceased due to a lack of capital being subscribed. Work was re-started, only to be brought to a halt again. In 1870 embarrassment was caused when the company's secretary, J. Bingham, was sentenced to twelve months' imprisonment with hard labour for attempting to defraud W. Baillie, the BNSR's Bristol banker. Works were then further delayed by heavy rain which caused landslides in the winter of 1871–2. The line eventually opened in 1873. In 1900, however, passenger ticket sales at Brislington station fell substantially, due to the opening of an electric tramway which siphoned off much of the traffic.

In 1958, after normal working hours, the branch was used for testing two rail bus chassis constructed by Bristol Commercial Vehicle Limited's works at Brislington, which was adjacent to the branch. Following rail trials over the branch line, the chassis were taken to Lowestoft by road where Eastern Coach Works fitted 56-seater bodies, similar to its bus design.

These vehicles did not prove successful because, although quite capable of carrying normal traffic, any significant increase in the number of passengers – say, on market day – meant that a normal-sized diesel multiple-unit had to be used and it would have been uneconomic to keep such a vehicle just for stand-by duty. Another reason for their lack of success was that freight services on branches they shared were withdrawn. Thus the freight's share of track upkeep was unavailable and income from the rail buses was insufficient to bear the total cost. Had they been developed 20 years earlier, the outcome could have been very different.

3

IMPROVEMENTS FOR BATH

It was a source of annoyance to Bath citizens that when they wished to travel northwards, a change at Temple Meads was required, and GWR trains to Bristol sometimes failed to provide a good connection with those of the MR to the north. A Midland Railway branch to Bath would avoid this inconvenience.

The main problem was the route. The GWR, being first in the field, had snatched the best so, to avoid constructing expensive bridges over the Avon, the MR would have to enter Bath at a higher level, with a station close to The Circus and Royal Crescent, both occupied by wealthy residents who were less than enamoured with the idea of the close proximity of a railway.

The alternative was a lower level route with six river bridges, but this was criticised by other inhabitants who feared that the river, which regularly flooded properties after prolonged rain or thaw, would be impeded by these crossings. The MR countered this complaint by demonstrating that the planned bridges would obstruct the water flow less than the existing structures.

On 6 July 1864, as the House of Lords Committee was discussing the MR's Bath Extension, the great cricketer W.G. Grace, then aged just 15, first played for the All-England Eleven against the Eighteen of Lansdown. This cricket match actually took place on Sydenham Field, later to become the site of the MR's Bath goods depot. As Lansdown Cricket Club's ground had to be sold to the MR, it relocated to a new site at Combe Park where play still takes place. Construction of the passenger terminus required the demolition of nine houses, while some homes in Albert Buildings, off the Lower Bristol Road, also had to be knocked down.

Vandalism was not unknown in Victorian times. In 1866 as the cutting at Bitton was being excavated, one day when the watchman was

The interior of Bath Midland Railway station c.1910. On the left is a hotel horse bus. (Author's collection)

absent, lads unchained and unbraked wagons and enjoyed a half-mile downhill ride.

That year the contractors employed 554 labourers and excavators, 85 artisans and 62 horses. In May 1866 the navvies were invited to 'an excellent tea, with beef, ham and plum cake' at a hall in Saltford. Following the meal they were urged to avoid public houses and strong drink, and instead to use the hall fitted up as a reading room.

On 3 August 1869, the day prior to the line's opening, disaster nearly struck at the new Bath station. A workman smelled gas, then used a naked light to locate its source. The resulting explosion blew out windows and forced a door off its hinges.

One curiosity at Bath was that although the rail distance between the MR's passenger and goods stations was only about 150 ft, the distance by road was a mile! In 1870 the MR constructed a bridge. It was opened to the public by courtesy only, a pair of gates at each end being closed at 11 pm.

Some of the streets approaching the station were narrow. A proprietary place of worship in Chapel Row was purchased to enable the road to be widened, while near Kingsmead Square, New Street was built to offer easier access from the city centre.

In October 1869 the Reverend W.E. Ray, of Bitton, sought permission to plant the slopes of the embankment opposite his home and for this privilege agreed to pay five shillings annually. In order to avoid any subsequent litigation, the MR safeguarded itself by stating that it would not be liable for any fire damage to plants.

The six lattice girder river bridges, although attractive, were not sufficiently strong to bear the weight of modern locomotives, so in the 1930s a replacement programme was initiated. In order not to halt traffic, Up and Down lines over a bridge were renewed separately, with a temporary signal box controlling trains over the single track section. As replacing the bridge outside of Bath station would have caused too much interruption to traffic, it was strengthened by welding at every joint. It still stands today.

Lines forming through routes were those which paid the best dividends. The Somerset & Dorset Railway (S&D) ran from Burnham-on-Sea to Poole. Unfortunately, passengers failed to utilise this facility. Looking for ways to

Bridge replacement at Newbridge, Bath, 1934. The plate girder span on the right has been replaced. The lattice girder span to its left will be replaced by the plate girder standing on the bank on the far left. This plate girder will be moved over the river to abut with the right-hand plate girder.
(Author's collection)

expand, the directors planned a route from Evercreech Junction, over the Mendip Hills to Bath, tapping collieries and stone quarries en route. One Bath schoolmaster used the excavations to observe the different rocks and note the varying botanical growth on them. The boys were particularly fascinated by 'stink stone', a rock with a pungent sulphur content found in Combe Down Tunnel.

Needing many tunnels, viaducts and substantial earthworks, the line was difficult to build and when finished, with gradients of 1 in 50, difficult to work. The Somerset Coal Canal tramway between Midford and Radstock was sold to the S&D for £15,000 cash and £5,000 paid-up shares.

Messrs Thomas & Charles Walker began the contract for building the extension in March 1872. That September two navvies were killed by a fall of earth near Devonshire Tunnel. In December 1873 three masons were standing on the arch of Midford Viaduct which spanned the Somerset Coal Canal when the arch cracked. Two of them fell through the hole and were killed when bricks fell on them. The third man jumped into the canal, but his injuries were not sufficient to prevent him walking the four miles to his lodgings in Bath.

Fatalities were not confined to men. In September 1872 one of Messrs Walker's horses was allowed to stray, fell into a cutting and broke its back. Unsurprisingly, 'the negligent servant decamped'.

In November 1872 some 110 navvies arrived at St Mark's School, Bath, 'to partake of some substantial fare'. Each man was given a plate of beef and potatoes 'of the most satisfying appearance' and as much tea, bread and plum pudding as he could eat.

On 12 June 1873 the two gangs which had commenced work on the Combe Down Tunnel over a mile apart and 15 months previously, met. Such was their accuracy that the meeting place could later only be discovered by observing the direction of the pick marks on the tunnel walls. Although probably his view was biased, W. Lean, Walker's district engineer, claimed that, although having been responsible for many tunnels, he considered the one at Combe Down his pet and claimed that there was not a better one in England. Nevertheless, on 13 December 1878 at approximately 7.30 am, about 20 tons of sand and stone caused the masonry to collapse near the tunnel's north portal, completely blocking the line. Fortunately the S&D, worried about the effect of severe frost on the tunnel, had employed two men to patrol it constantly, so the fall was discovered before a train could plough into it. Horse brakes were ordered and used to convey passengers and luggage between Bath and Midford for the rest of the day. Work on strengthening the tunnel walls was still in progress at least until March 1879.

Class 2P 4-4-0 No 40563 and West Country class Pacific No 34044 Woolacombe burst from Combe Down Tunnel with a Down train, 18 July 1953. (R.E. Toop)

Approximately a thousand men were engaged on building the 26½-mile-long line and it was to the great credit of Messrs Walker that such a difficult line was opened on 20 July 1874, having taken only just over two years to construct.

4

RUNNING THE RAILWAYS

Railway companies, like many other organisations, were arranged in departments. Some dealt with the actual operation: station staff, engineering, signalling, permanent way, locomotives, carriages and wagons. Other departments dealt with the commercial aspects, such as advertising, property maintenance and employment of staff.

Generally, a railwayman started as a lad in one of the departments and if capable, rose up the ladder through the various grades – a goods porter might end up as a yard foreman. Promotion from one step to the next was generally determined by length of service but when a railwayman left his base grade he was also expected to acquire a good deal of specialised knowledge. For instance, a train guard was required to know the company's rules and regulations and be able to locate the position of signal boxes, signals and gradients on various routes.

A driver started as a cleaner – which meant that he became intimate with the various parts of a locomotive. In addition to cleaning, he might be assigned to other tasks, such as assisting a boiler smith or a firebox brick-arch repairer. Another duty was that of 'call boy' – essential in the days when most households had only one clock and there were no such things as time checks on the radio. A call boy went to their house and knocked a driver, fireman or guard up an hour before he was required to sign on.

The system usually worked well but things could go wrong. One day when Guard Frank Staddon of 12 Edward Street, Bath, arrived at work, he was told that Control would not let him sign on, claiming that a call boy had visited him three times and that on each occasion Frank had failed to answer. Frank strongly denied this and said that no one had called. Control relented and allowed him to sign on to work. When he returned home later that day, neighbour Mr Smith of 2 Edward Street told Frank that during the night vandals had kicked his door and it bore the marks of a hob-nailed boot. Frank asked Mr Smith to write a letter to the LMS claiming compensation for damage to his door and for being unnecessarily roused. It transpired that the reason the call boy went to the wrong house was that the figure '1' on his sheet was indistinct.

A cleaner was tested and, if successful, became a Passed Cleaner, that is, he could be called upon for firing duty. After 313 firing days (a year minus 52 rest days) he was paid a fireman's rate whether he was firing or cleaning. At Bath the shed was only busy in the summer months, so some Bath cleaners anxious to rise up the ladder transferred in winter to busier sheds in order to accumulate more firing duties and thus be fixed on the higher rate of pay.

The progress of an aspiring footplateman was usually:

Cleaner
Passed Cleaner (i.e. passed for firing duty)
Fireman
Registered Fireman (i.e. covered a minimum of 313 firing turns)
Passed Fireman (i.e. passed for driving duty)
Driver
Registered Driver (i.e. covered a minimum of 313 driving turns)

The next grades on the ladder were supervisory and their occupants known as Inspectors. Such posts were open not only to those who had worked up through the lower grades, but also to members of the clerical staff whose standard of education was to School Certificate level. Promotion to a supervisory position was determined by suitability. Graduates entering the traffic departments were given the same special course of training as traffic apprentices.

THE LOCOMOTIVES

Locomotive depots are of prime importance on a railway. The work of a steam locomotive depot fell into two main divisions: that of maintaining engines in good repair and that of arranging for suitable engines and footplate staff to be available and out at the times required by the operating department.

Repairs carried out at the depot could be described as running repairs, while periodic general overhauls and heavy repairs were sent to either Swindon, Derby, Crewe or Horwich, depending whether it was a GWR or an LMS engine.

Good maintenance was vital, as engine failures in traffic had extremely serious consequences in delay to trains, which might mean that passengers or goods would seek alternative routes in future. It was especially important that mail

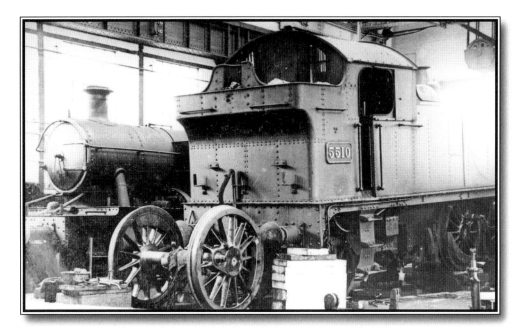

*The rear set of driving wheels have been removed from 4575 class 2-6-2T
No 5510 at Bath Road shed, 25 April 1936. (Author's collection)*

trains kept to time, whatever the weather; in 1950 Driver Tommy King was sent a few minutes ahead of the 7.20 pm mail train from Temple Meads to the North on a class 2P 4-4-0, fitted with a snow plough to ensure that no drifts impeded the following train.

A locomotive shed superintendent arranged the provision of engines and crews and supervised staff responsible for the duties of fire-dropping, stabling and preparing engines for boiler washing and tube cleaning. He was required to deal with cases of bad running, ascertain their cause and report on them, whether it be failure on the part of personnel or of materials. He was also responsible for operating the breakdown crane when an accident made it necessary for one to be sent out. Despatching an engine into traffic was not always as simple as it first appeared, involving detailed arrangements relating to the locomotives and to the footplate staff.

The staff compiling the locomotive workings needed to have an exact knowledge of the type of engine suitable for each train and the number of locomotives of each type allocated to that shed. The depot superintendent was responsible for ensuring that a suitable engine left the shed to fit in with the timetabled departure time from the station or goods yard.

For economy it was necessary to secure the highest possible number of hours in steam. It was most desirable to double-shift engines, that is, to work them for two turns a day, as one engine could work for two shifts at considerably less cost than two engines working one shift each.

Duties of enginemen were organised in the form of a roster, which was sub-divided into 'links', arranged on a seniority basis. They started with engine preparation and disposal within the depot yard, then progress was made to shunting and with local freight, long-distance freight, local passenger and finally express passenger. In each link the men worked round weekly, thus sharing equally the early and late turns.

The first GWR locomotive shed at Bristol was near the site of the later South Wales Junction. Initially a three-road building, a four-road shed was added later. Shortly after the opening of the line between Bristol and Bath in 1840, it was the scene of an amusing mishap: east of Temple Meads, a train of 'nine crowded coaches', instead of taking the main line, was inadvertently diverted into the engine shed sidings. The driver shut off steam and the guards applied their brakes. The *Bath Chronicle* reported: 'The harsh grating sound occasioned by the sudden application of the breaks [sic], gave the first intimation to the passengers that something was wrong. As alarm soon spread from carriage to carriage, the inquiry had scarcely been made "What's the matter?" when the train engine 2-2-2 *Lynx*, collided with *Arrow* of the same class.'

The *Bath & Cheltenham Gazette* continues the story: 'The concussion was such as to bring the parties sitting opposite each other so closely in contact, that several of them sustained violent blows. As might be imagined, the fears of the travellers got the better of their judgments, and most gave their lungs full play, in which harmonic exercise the fair sex by no means played "second fiddle". Besides injuries due to the ladies' bonnets and other articles of their dress of similar fragile texture, a very few pounds will put it all right.' 'The "switch man",' the report went on, 'deemed it prudent to "make himself scarce" at the Station, yesterday morning.'

One driver, on arrival at Bristol St Philip's with a passenger train from Bath, uncoupled his engine and was running round. He failed to notice an open catch point and running over it, the engine was derailed. Knowing that this error would lead to punishment, he immediately thought of an excuse. Removing the pressure gauge glass protection, he shattered the glass. He was then able to falsely claim that the gauge glass had broken, distracting his attention from the road and therefore causing the derailment. His excuse was not accepted and he received two days' suspension.

St Philip's caused problems for another driver. One foggy, frosty morning the

Class 3P 2-6-2T No 40174 is drawing forward at Bristol St Philip's, while detaching a van, c.1950. (Author's collection)

disc signal indicating the position of the points failed to come off. The driver walked to the signalman and informed him that the disc was not quite clear. The signalman pulled the lever repeatedly and asked the driver to move forward. He did … and the engine came off the road. A crane had to be called to re-rail it and then the engine inspected to ensure that nothing had been damaged. This meant a trip to Derby for the driver and fireman to explain the circumstances to Colonel Rudgard, the LMS Line Superintendent. He accepted their excuse.

Smart drivers had ways of making life easier: Bert Shipp of Bath used markers. The locomotive turntables at Bath and St Philip's were manually operated and unless an engine was exactly balanced on the table, it was impossible to turn. When running onto a turntable, most drivers sent their fireman down to call out when an engine was about to make the turntable go down, thus indicating that it was balanced, but not so Bert Shipp. He used a marker and knew that when he was alongside it, then the table was perfectly balanced.

Midland engines were right-hand drive and if a water column was on the right-hand side, it was easy to see where to stop, but if it was on the left-hand side, it was more difficult. Here, too, Bert had an easy solution – a marker such as an advertisement, railway post, or a nick on the platform edge.

Not all drivers owned a watch; in fact, sometimes the first they had was the one given to them on retirement! Driver Fred Holmes, for instance, said that if the company had wished him to have a watch, it would have supplied him with one. Many drivers used their judgment, or the station or church clock to keep time. When in charge of a goods train, one driver said that he looked down at the sleeper ends and if he could count them, he knew that he was going too slowly and would lose time.

A good driver was very observant at all times and noticed the slightest unusual thing about his engine. He had an inbuilt habit that whenever his locomotive stopped, he would walk round and gently rub the palm of his hand against each big end to check that nothing was exceptionally warm; that no cork had come out of a side rod oil filler; and that no trimming was incorrect.

Tea could not be made on an engine, so it was the last job before leaving a depot to make a brew. There was always a big pot of hot water in a locoman's cabin. When made, the tea was kept warm in a can on a tray above the firebox door. Eggs, bacon and mushrooms could be fried on a shovel. Firstly, the slacking pipe producing water at high pressure was used to clean the shovel and then it was plunged into the firebox to dry. Fat was placed on the shovel followed by the food. One minute was sufficient. Cooking could only be carried out when an engine was stationary – if moving, the blast would have whisked the food off the shovel. Similarly, you avoided turning on the blower if your mate was cooking, or again the food would have vanished up the chimney.

The footplate crew washed in a bucket. Booking on, they drew from the stores a bucket holding five spanners, a hammer and a sealed canister approximately 10 in by 4 in containing flags and detonators for use if the train failed, or fouled the opposite line. If that happened a fireman went forward and protected the opposite line by putting down detonators: one at a quarter of a mile, one at half a mile, and three, ten yards apart, at one mile. He carried a red flag and walked along the line to the nearest signal box, or track-circuited signal, where he could phone. The guard similarly protected the train's rear.

Footplate men could be relied on to be safe because they had so many tests for health and eyesight. If they failed, they were taken off driving or firing, or transferred to less important duties such as shunting or banking.

A good fireman tried to prevent the engine's safety valves blowing off, because 20 gallons a minute could be lost and apart from the loss of water, it meant that he had shovelled coal to heat that water to no purpose. One way of preventing blowing off was to turn on the injector to bring cold water into the boiler and thus lower its temperature.

Firing an engine was not just a matter of flinging coal into the firebox, it required careful placing so that the fire was not too thin at the front, or too thick at the back. Although the condition of the rear of the fire could usually be seen, observation of the front was more difficult. The trick was to use a shovel as a reflector or deflector. The back of the shovel was used as a mirror – the flame reflecting on the shovel as it was moved around in a semi-circle. Turning the blade over would deflect the incoming air and take the flame off the top of the fire just momentarily while the fireman took a fleeting glance.

A steam locomotive took a great deal of time to be prepared. Apart from lubricating its moving parts, steam could not be raised instantly. The steam raiser lit an engine up about eight hours before she was needed to go into traffic. He threw about 8 cwt of coal into the firebox, leaving a space in the centre beneath the fire hole door. Then he added half a dozen firelighters, with another dozen lumps of coal on top, left the damper open, closed the firebox door and left her to her own devices. Black smoke poured out through the cracks around the door and it could take four hours before she began to generate steam. The steam raiser would occasionally return and add a few more lumps to the fire. He was not concerned about making a lot of steam, as long as he raised 40–50 lb before the engine was due out for traffic he had done his job and the rest was the responsibility of the crew.

One of the last things to do before leaving an engine shed was to top up the coal and water. A largish engine such as a Jubilee or Black Five used water at the rate of 35 to 40 gallons a minute and 50 lb of coal per mile – the exact amount depending on the weight and speed of the train, gradients and the condition of the engine.

Different types of coal demanded different firing techniques. North coal as used by the MR/LMS at Bristol could be shovelled into the firebox of a stationary engine. Welsh coal on the other hand should only have been placed on by hand because it was slow-combustion coal; it was also dusty and required a greater supply of primary air through the ashpan. Welsh dust would only ignite when the fire was burning well. Bedwas coal was the favourite – no clinker was made, so at the end of the day the ashpan could be raked and any dust fell into the ashbox. MR/LMS engines had a 'married man's tender'; that is, it saved strain on a fireman's back as the coal came out at, or above, the firebox door height. GWR engines had a 'single man's tender' – he had to lift the coal from the tender floor to the fire hole.

Firemen needed to be ambidextrous because drivers preferred their mate to fire from the side opposite them, which meant that a right-hand drive engine needed to be fired left-handed. One driver actually drew a line across the centre

Raking out the ashpan of BR Standard class 9 2-10-0 No 92214, c.1960 at Bath, Green Park shed. (Dr T.R.N. Edwards)

of the footplate and warned his fireman never to cross it. S&D class 7F 2-8-0s Nos 13800–5 were right-hand drive, while the remainder of the class, Nos 13806–10, had left-hand drive.

Bath Road shed (BRD in GWR code; 82A in BR code) was originally a six-road broad gauge B&E depot adjoining the locomotive works. In later days it became mixed gauge. When the rail improvements were made in the Bristol area in the early 1930s, the shed was rebuilt. The main building, 210 ft by 167 ft and constructed of brick with a slated roof, had ten roads; beside it was a three-road repair shop 170 ft by 50 ft, similarly of brick with a slated roof. A coal stage surmounted by a 135,000 gallon water tank separated the two buildings.

The water came from the River Avon via Fox's Wood pumping station, which also supplied St Philip's Marsh shed, Fox's Wood water troughs, and water for carriage washing and cleaning cattle pens. Although the water was generally of reasonable quality, spring tides could cause slight salt contamination and thus lead to boiler priming – that is, throwing water from the chimney.

A busy time at Bath Road depot, 7 June 1952. All the shed roads are occupied. (R.E. Toop)

The original location of Fox's Wood troughs, 27 June 1896 to 30 October 1898.
(Author's collection)

Overfilling the boiler was another cause of priming. One fine summer's day in the 1930s this happened near the Bath LMS shed. An engine passed over Victoria Bridge Road just as a lady dressed in a light summer frock was about to pass underneath. The black, sooty water did not improve her appearance. She wrote to the stationmaster and the railway company paid her cleaning expenses.

It is not always appreciated by the layman that steam locomotives needed to take on water more frequently than coal. Fox's Wood water troughs east of St Anne's Park enabled engines to pick up water on the move. They were first used on 27 June 1896 when Achilles class 4-2-2 No 3042 *Frederick Saunders* headed a non-stop special carrying the Prince of Wales from Cardiff to Paddington. Rather surprisingly the troughs were taken out of use on 30 October 1898. It is thought that this was due to the fact that they were partly situated in a tunnel and water splashing from an over-full tender on to the sooty walls and then bouncing back on to the coaches, particularly those with open

4-6-0 No 5027 Farleigh Castle *passes Keynsham troughs with an Up stopping train 3 April 1956. The water tank is on the left.* (R.E. Toop)

windows, could have had serious consequences. New troughs nearer Keynsham were opened on 30 June 1899. With the decreasing number of steam engines using them, they were taken out of use in May 1961.

On 6 October 1940 a bomb destroyed the filter, so water was pumped direct, resulting in an eel spending three years in a 0-6-0PT's water tank. The pump, originally steam-powered, was latterly worked by electricity. In the event of the latter failing, a bell was rung automatically at the Bath Road shed. Bath Road

closed to steam on 12 September 1960, its stock of locomotives being transferred to St Philip's Marsh and Barrow Road.

St Philip's Marsh depot (SPM, later 82B) opened on 9 July 1910, chiefly supplying goods engines and leaving Bath Road to concentrate on passenger locomotives. St Philip's Marsh also provided mixed traffic engines such as Halls and Granges for the many summer Saturday North to West holiday trains using the conveniently adjacent Bristol Avoiding Line; engines or crews being changed near the shed. Many drivers preferred a Grange to a Hall class locomotive.

On bank holidays extra trains were run to Weston-super-Mare. These usually consisted of ten coach formations, sometimes made up to eleven. Here drivers would rather have a Pannier tank 0-6-0, than a 45XX class 2-6-2T – only the six driving wheels took the full weight of the engine, which gave better adhesion than a 2-6-2T where the locomotive's weight was spread over the two pony trucks as well.

When Bath Road was short of power, it requested the loan of a 'Marsh' engine and if in recent ex-factory condition, it was not unusual for them to keep it until either it needed repair, or a boiler wash-out, when it would then be sent home.

St Philip's Marsh was the second largest depot on the GWR system, the largest being at Old Oak Common. Built of brick with a slated roof, it measured 246 ft by 364 ft. Twenty-eight roads radiated from each of the two turntables. A roundhouse built round a turntable had the advantage that when a driver was oiling an engine, particularly if he was reaching to the inside motion, his engine could never be struck, causing the motion to move and thus threatening him with injury or death. A roundhouse also had the advantage over a straight shed in that it was easy to abstract a particular engine without having to move others. The only serious disadvantage was that if the turntable broke down, all the engines inside were trapped. During the Second World War the allocation of locomotives at the Marsh reached 199; if one more had been given, the chief foreman would have been granted a higher grade.

St Philip's Marsh locomotive depot: 4-6-0 No 6954 Lotherton Hall *is near the coaling stage awaiting replenishment, April 1964. Coal wagons stand on a siding at a higher level. A water tank forms the coaling stage roof.*
(W.F. Grainger)

A steel-framed extension to the shed was added later for the maintenance of GWR diesel railcars by AEC fitters, GWR cleaners only wiping their bodywork with cleaning oil. Below the 145,000 gallon water tank was a two-road coal stage. The depot closed on 13 June 1964 when its few remaining engines were transferred to Barrow Road.

St Philip's Marsh saw some surprising visitors. A Southern Railway B4 class 0-4-0T which had been withdrawn when replaced at Southampton Docks by the United States' War Department 0-6-0Ts, was seen one Saturday morning in the late 1940s on the coaling road. It had arrived via Salisbury under its own steam and was being coaled en route to its new industrial owners in South Wales. Being in steam and not 'dead', it was allowed through the Severn Tunnel. Later, in the 1948 freight locomotive interchange trials between Bristol and Eastleigh, the WD 2-10-0, LNER B1 class 4-6-0, LMS class 5 4-6-0, SR West Country Pacific No 34006 *Bude* and, of course, the GWR 28XX class 2-8-0 were to be seen. Several of the remaining Aberdare class 2-6-0s also made their final journey through here to Swindon. Indeed, one travelled to Swindon on only one cylinder, the other side being disconnected due to slipped eccentric sheaves. A fitter travelled on the footplate with a pinch bar so that in the event of it not starting, he could place it below a wheel and lever it forwards.

In 1873 the small Bristol & Gloucester Railway two-road locomotive depot adjacent to the GWR shed at South Wales Junction, was replaced by a standard brick-built roundhouse. This shed, known as Barrow Road, was given the MR code 8; LMS 22A and BR 82E.

In 1935 when LMS motive power depots were reorganised into locomotive supply concentration and garage schemes, Barrow Road became a main,

Barrow Road locomotive depot, 19 April 1965. Left to right: ex-LMS class 8F 2-8-0 No 48409 (built by the GWR at Swindon), a steam crane and BR Standard class 5 4-6-0 No 73003. (R.E. Toop)

or concentration depot, with Gloucester, Bath/Radstock, Templecombe, Highbridge, Tewkesbury and Wells as garage depots. This scheme introduced economy by reducing the necessity of stocking parts at garage depots. Barrow Road was well-equipped with a wheel drop pit, a wheel lathe, two sheer-legs for lifting, and a coaling tower permitting two engines to be coaled simultaneously. There was also an ash disposal plant, while in 1927, a 60-ft-diameter turntable replaced one of 46 ft. The LMS, unlike the GWR, was able to coal mechanically because it used North coal which was hard, whereas the GWR used soft Welsh coal which would have broken too easily. The mechanical coal hopper, however, proved a problem on one occasion. One loaded coal wagon was not checked before its contents were tipped into the hopper. It was full of pipes, not coal! Their removal from the hopper proved difficult and time-consuming.

Italian prisoners of war were employed at Barrow Road during the Second World War. They lived in the ambulance hut and laboured in the yard. Times were hard and they were remembered for trapping starlings to eat and the fact that they made stew from cat food.

The Bristol Port Railway & Pier (BPRP) during its 25 years of independent existence had only two locomotive superintendents. The first was a man named Miller, a Bristolian who on leaving the company's service went to Peru. The second was J. Keefe, who was appointed by the Receiver and stayed until the line was taken over by the Clifton Extension Railway. The single road engine shed was at Shirehampton.

The stone-built, two-road Midland Railway shed opened at Bath in 1869. Its MR code was 8 – the same as Bristol; then LMS 22C. In 1948 it became Southern Region 71G and finally Western Region 82F in 1958. The shed closed on 7 March 1966. Outside were a 42-ft-diameter turntable and a coal stage constructed of timber. As this shed would have proved quite inadequate to cater for locomotives when the Somerset & Dorset's Bath Extension opened, the MR constructed a two-road shed, 160 ft by 30 ft, from timber and set it near the boat wharf.

Ten years later the coal stage, constructed of timber and brick, was converted into a fitters' and blacksmiths' shop. This new engine shed proved inadequate for the number of S&D locomotives requiring to use it, so an almost identical building was added alongside, occupying the site of the MR turntable. Its replacement was larger – 46 ft in diameter. This was replaced in 1935 by one of 60 ft. Whenever the Bath turntable was out of action, it was the practice to run locomotives to Mangotsfield to turn on the triangular junction. In order to avoid too much line occupation on such occasions, several engines, sometimes as many as four, proceeded there coupled together.

View of Bath LMS locomotive depot c.1935. The timber-built S&D shed is in the centre and the stone-built MR shed centre right. (Author's collection)

The S&D shed finally measured 300 ft by 60 ft and each of the four roads had a pit the length of the shed. Artificial lighting progressed from tallow candles to oil 'duck' lamps (so called because they had the appearance of ducks), gas flames, gas fan burners, gas mantles and for the final five years, electricity. Fire precautions for this highly combustible structure consisted of boiler washing-out hoses and numerous buckets of water hanging on the shed walls. The fitting shop received electricity in 1909 to power the dc motor to drive three lathes, two drillers, a shaper and grindstone through overhead shafts and belts.

The office and stores at the S&D shed were built piece by piece. The timber was obtained from the S&D works at Highbridge for 'wagon repairs' and then stored until the quantity was sufficient for a part of the building to be erected. The chimney was constructed from bricks really intended for locomotive firebox arches, while the gas lamps were second-hand from Highbridge Works.

As the shed was not far above river level, it occasionally flooded. The shed's water supply came from a spring in the S&D's Devonshire Tunnel. Bath water was hard, so in 1938 a water softener was erected. Sludge from the softener was pumped into an old tender and when full was sent to Coalville, Leicestershire. There were two such tenders: one ready to be filled while the other was emptied. LMS engines were fitted with continuous blowdown valves so that when the regulator was open, a small quantity of water was continuously drained from the boiler. This had the effect of keeping down the surface scum formed by the chemical action of the softened water and therefore helped to prevent priming.

Although the quantity of water lost via a blowdown valve was relatively small – one to one and a half gallons a minute – a driver whose engine was shy on steam would use a ploy to avoid this loss. He unscrewed a nut, removed the blowdown valve and inserted a farthing or sixpence before replacing it. This stopped any water from being ejected.

Some of the locomotive sidings adjacent to the shed were built unofficially. The foundations were ashes from the drop pits; the permanent way was obtained from the Engineer's Department, paid for by the exchange of drivers' and firemen's second-hand overcoats which were then, unofficially, distributed to gangers and packers.

The Great Western Railway engine shed at Bath was a very puny structure compared with that of the LMS. In the early days it was a single road affair of timber with a slated roof, adjacent to the passenger platform. In November 1880 a single road shed, probably mixed gauge, was opened at the Westmoreland Road goods yard. Its brick walls were partly concealed by cast-

The entrance to the GWR's Bath Road locomotive depot. The notice on the door reads: 'Great Western Railway. No Admittance Except On Business. By Order.'
(Michael Jenkins)

4575 class 2-6-2T No 5528 at the ex-GWR locomotive shed at Bath, 1949. A water tank forms the shed roof. (Author's collection)

iron columns supporting the water tank that formed the roof. In fact, looking at it, one saw the tank rather than the shed.

At one time two steam railmotors and a shunting engine were allocated to this Bath shed, but latterly it was just the 0-6-0PT used for shunting. The final 0-6-0PT left the shed on 13 May 1961 and until the shed's closure on 5 February 1966, it was occupied by a diesel shunter.

Rolling stock

The distribution of rolling stock differed depending on whether it was for passenger or goods use. Passengers generally travelled in approximately equal numbers in each direction between any two points, although on a particular day the flow might happen to be unequal. Apart from odd vehicles added to passenger trains to meet an exceptional demand, a railway company therefore had to arrange its carriage working on the general basis of running trains in each direction with sufficient capacity to hold the peak number of passengers. This meant that empty seats had to be hauled, to a greater or lesser extent. Sometimes this waste of capacity could be mitigated by reducing the number of carriages at certain times of the day or week. Another ploy was to try and fill them by offering cheap fares at certain times.

Although some goods stations had a more or less balanced traffic inwards and outwards, it was by no means invariably so. Even when it was roughly balanced, the outwards and inwards traffic often required different types of wagons. For example, the banana traffic from Avonmouth needed very specialised heated vans and could not, say, be carried in wagons which had brought domestic or gas coal to Bristol.

The distribution of empty goods wagons was organised on a simple plan. Each station was required to report daily to the district operating office in Bristol, stating the number of wagons which it required for loading, the number of empty wagons it had on hand, and the surplus or further requirements in empty wagons. The districts then reported in summary form to the divisional office where, each evening, decisions were made on the empty wagons to be moved between districts.

Special instructions related to the distribution of freight train brake vans, as any errors in distribution could result in serious delay to trains. The GWR vans bore the name of their home base, so any out-of-course vans could be returned.

Many stations had a repair road. For instance, the Midland goods yard at Bath had a Cripple Dock where up to 30 wagons daily with damaged doors, sides, axle boxes, drawbars and buffers were put back into running order.

COACHES

Today when vehicles are used so intensively, it is not always realised that this was not the way in the past. In steam days, coaches of express trains were often taken away for cleaning at the end of each trip. Then there were the many extra coaches required for summer Saturday trains, some making only perhaps six or so journeys a year. There were also sets needed for excursions or works outings, while coaches had to be made available to strengthen a train if traffic proved to be heavy; perhaps even a duplicate would be run.

By 1878 there was a carriage shed at each end of Temple Meads station. Due to the constriction of space caused by the river bridges, both sheds were set at right angles to the main lines with access by turntable.

A newspaper advertisement from 5 January 1934 for cheap LMS excursions from Bath.

Dr Day's Carriage Sidings, named after a beloved GP and railway doctor who lived near the sidings, were sited between the LMS and GWR lines, and built under a 1930 government loan, as were those at Malago Vale. Marsh Pond Sidings east of St Philip's Marsh opened in 1917 for storing non-corridor and excursion stock. Other sidings for storing passenger stock were at Ashton Gate, Filton West Junction, Bristol West Sidings and Pylle Hill.

The MR carriage shed was at Barrow Road and involved backing twelve coach trains for about a mile from Barrow Road to Platform 13 at Temple Meads, this platform being a terminus. The route the coaches took was over busy junctions, with just a shunter in the leading coach

Temple Meads: on a summer's day permanent way gangers are at work in the foreground, while a carriage shed is seen to the left.
(Author's collection)

giving hand signals – a procedure which was carried out quite successfully. Other LMS coaches were stored at Mangotsfield North Junction.

The GWR's oil gas plant at Bristol was on the east side of the Bath Road complex, the works supplying fuel for lighting buildings and yards, while gas was piped to Marsh Pond, Dr Day's and Malago Vale for supplying coach lighting and for cooking in restaurant cars. Boys were employed to 'gas up' coaches and had to tolerate the stink clinging to their hands and clothes. Rail tank wagons were sent to stations in the area to replenish the coach gas tanks of vehicles used on branch lines and which did not normally come to Bristol.

The LMS had a gas plant at St Philip's, but to effect a saving of £350 a year, the works were closed in 1934 and gas purchased from the GWR's plant. An empty gas tank wagon left Bath LMS station every Monday on the 12.17 pm passenger train to Bristol to be recharged – the gas was needed for the restaurant car on the Pines Express.

At its opening, BPRP passenger trains comprised twelve coaches and two passenger brake vans, all four-wheelers. On the opening day passengers commented approvingly that the vehicles rode steadily. Its first passenger livery was yellow and white. Probably this colour scheme proved difficult to keep clean and later the composite coaches were painted dark chocolate while the remainder of the stock was stained and grained.

Well into the 20th century, coaches for use by Avonmouth dockers had wooden seats which were more hygienic than the upholstered kind, but bugs were found even on wooden seats. If dockers were found sitting on upholstered seats, they were politely, but firmly, told to get off and sit on the wooden ones. Dockers had a habit of spitting on the windows so not surprisingly the coaches were rather dirty.

ALWAYS IN DANGER

As the 9 pm Bath to Bristol train approached Kelston on 10 November 1887, the driver suddenly realised that his fireman, John Knight, aged 24, was missing. He stopped immediately and Knight was found lying a short distance behind the train. He was unconscious, with severe injuries to his head that seemed to indicate having come into contact with the wall of the bridge close to where he was lying.

The driver of the passing Bristol to Bath train stopped and took the injured man to Bath where he was carried to the Royal United Hospital. It was found that his skull was fractured in two places and his body bruised. He died the following day. At the inquest it was decided that Knight, reaching for either his pricker or dart, kept at the side of the engine, had overbalanced and fallen.

Ambulance Brigade.

Photo by) G.W.R. (BATH) AMBULANCE SECTION. (Toogood.
H. G. Arnold Sergt. W. A. Ravesteyn
(capt. of team). (drill instructor).
E. J. Bust. T. England. F. C. Hitchcock. F. Hancock.

The GWR's St John Ambulance Brigade at Bath, April 1904. (Toogood)

It was no accident that many railwaymen were trained first-aiders. There was plenty of scope on the railways for getting injured. Fires could blow back into the cab or a gauge glass could burst. To enable a footplate man hanging outside the cab to turn the steam off, some GWR engines had a cock handle situated outside the cab.

Shunting was also fraught with danger – men could trip over a rail and have a limb amputated by a wagon, or be crushed between buffers. Fogmen could be killed when placing a detonator on the line. One did get killed at Yatton and the parsimonious company insisted that as the overcoat supplied to him was still in good condition – apart from the bloodstains – it should continue to be worn. Men working on the permanent way might miss spotting an approaching train – in fact, this happened to the uncle of one of my distant relations.

On 20 March 1879 the 12.15 pm from Wimborne had to stop at the home signal at Bath Junction. Driver Henry Bullard used the opportunity to climb down to examine his engine to make sure that everything was running in good order. He was horrified to discover a boot and part of a man's foot attached to a sand pipe. When he arrived at Bath station he informed the locomotive foreman. A search party left immediately on an engine commandeered from a goods train. Almost midway through Combe Down Tunnel, 36-year-old permanent way man Frederick Francis was found with both legs severely damaged and a badly injured hand. Conscious, he held the hand of one of the men who had discovered him and said: 'It's a bad job. I don't know what happened.' He was taken to the Royal United Hospital, then situated in Lower Borough Walls, only a quarter of a mile from the Midland station. He was admitted at 4.40 pm and died 25 minutes later, leaving a widow and six children.

A gang of about 20 men had been employed repairing the tunnel walls only 618 yards away from Frederick Francis, but were quite unaware of the incident. This gang was protected by three watchmen who laid a detonator on the track and drivers also whistled a warning, so a train's approach was certainly audible. Frederick had an entirely separate duty, which was tightening fishplate bolts and he was working by himself. He was sober and not deaf, so must have been aware of the train's approach, especially as the engine was working up a gradient of 1 in 100. Manholes were available where he could have taken refuge and even if these were not used, where he was found there was a space of 2 ft 9 in between the train and the tunnel wall. One manhole was 28 yards away on one side of him and 32 yards on the other. At the inquest Joseph Lowe, permanent way inspector from Shepton Mallet, said: 'The pressure of the air and the vibration of a hand lamp would tell anyone that a train was in the tunnel.' While it is possible that he was fully aware of the presence of the train, but had left a tool where it could have been damaged and was struck trying to rescue it, the accident remained inexplicable.

5

BRISTOL'S LOCOMOTIVES

Bristol is famous for so many things that it is not always appreciated that locomotive building was an important industry in the city. In fact, between 1864 and 1881 no fewer than one in nine locomotives constructed in Britain were made in Bristol, and between 1837 and 1958 it built about 4,200.

The first locomotive works in the city was started in 1837 by Henry Asprey Stothert, son of George Stothert who owned the Bath foundry which eventually became Stothert & Pitt. Stothert built locomotives for, among others, the GWR, B&E and S&D, providing good machines at low prices. In 1839 he took Edward Slaughter, one of Brunel's assistants, on as partner. To keep the workforce busy when demand for locomotives was slack, they also manufactured marine engines, steam pumps and point capstans. Stothert having retired, in 1856 Henry Gruning joined the firm which then became Slaughter, Gruning & Company. In late 1865 it was restyled the Avonside Engine Company, it being located at Avonside Wharf.

That year the firm constructed 20 broad gauge 2-4-0 locomotives of the Hawthorn class for the GWR, one having the name *Slaughter*. Seeing that such a nameplate would do little to instil confidence in passengers, a railway director insisted on it being renamed *Avonside*. In 1871, under licence, the firm built articulated engines to the design of Robert Fairlie, and locomotives of this pattern successfully worked on the Festiniog Railway. By the mid-1870s the firm was employing 800 to 900 men and constructing about one locomotive a week, but due to a depression in trade, the firm was liquidated in July 1881, throwing the men out of work.

In August 1882 Edwin Walker purchased Avonside's machinery, patterns and spares, and leased part of the works for locomotive construction. As early as

1902 the company built an internal combustion-engined locomotive for use in the Transvaal. The firm flourished, continuing to build steam engines and in 1904 Walker took on Ronald Murray as a partner. It was he who provided the capital for the construction of a new works at Fishponds, where a maximum workforce of 300 was employed. The Depression, however, caused the firm to go into liquidation on 29 November 1934 and it closed early in 1935. Between 1841 and 1935 the firm had built 1,960 engines – an average of 21 annually. The company's goodwill, drawings, patterns and spares were acquired by the Hunslet Engine Company of Leeds.

Meanwhile, in 1864 two Quakers, Francis William Fox (the cousin of Francis Fox, B&E engineer) and Edwin Walker, jointly founded Fox, Walker & Company with the object of specialising in the construction of industrial locomotives. Fox was responsible for the financial side and Walker the engineering aspect. The works were in Deep Pit Road, St George, adjacent to the Midland Railway and actually accessed via a colliery branch. Between 1864 and 1878 the factory was known as the Atlas Engineering Works.

The company hoped to make a fortune with the Steep Gradient Locomotive patented by Henry Handyside in 1873 and tested during the construction of Avonmouth Docks. This engine was able to climb a gradient of 1 in 10 by gripping a centre rail. Unfortunately, the idea failed to become popular and due to a falling demand for locomotive building, the firm was wound up in December 1878. In 1881 the Atlas Engineering Works was taken over by Thomas Peckett, who continued building industrial locomotives.

Peckett's survived the Depression, but in the late 1940s kept to steam and failed to change over to building diesel locomotives, which by then most industrial users required. By 1956 when the firm eventually started building internal-combustion powered locomotives, it was too late, its customers had bought elsewhere.

The last steam engine built in Bristol was a tank engine completed in June 1958 for a Mozambique sugar estate. The very last locomotive left the works in February 1961 when the firm was taken over by the Reed Crane & Hoist Company Limited. Some 2,166 locomotives had been built since 1864 – an average of just over 22 annually.

In addition to these private locomotive builders, the Bristol & Exeter's locomotive works opened in January 1852 on a site which later became Bath Road Locomotive Depot. Initially the works was just used for overhauling engines, but it built its first locomotive in 1859 and completed a further 34 during the ensuing 16 years. As the company's main line was only 76 miles in length, it tended to use tank engines. One express passenger class was a most

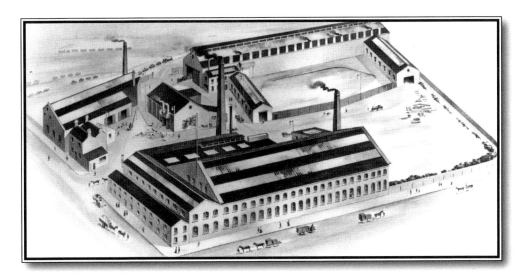

Bird's eye view of Peckett's Atlas Locomotive Works. (Author's collection)

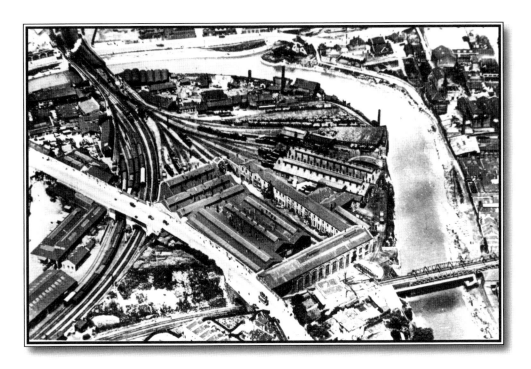

Aerial view of the former B&E locomotive works, Bath Road, Bristol, c.1930.
(M.J. Tozer collection)

impressive 4-2-4T, with 8 ft 10 in diameter flangeless driving wheels, reaching to almost the top of the boiler. B&E No 41, equipped with these wheels, the largest in regular use in Britain, achieved a record speed of 81.8 mph down Wellington Bank in June 1854, this remaining for 36 years as the highest authenticated speed record.

Express passenger 4-2-4T, as GWR No 2002, built by the B&E at Bristol, 1873. (Author's collection)

A factory concerned with another aspect of railway production was the Bristol Wagon & Carriage Works. In 1851 two Quakers, John Fowler and Albert Fry, began making agricultural implements in Temple Street. Five years later when Fowler left to establish his own firm in Leeds, Fry took on his cousin Theodore as partner. Theodore left in 1866 and the Bristol Wagon Works was formed to take over the business with Albert Fry as managing director. A factory was built beside the Midland Railway at Lawrence Hill, with a siding connection.

In 1869 the firm was renamed the Bristol Wagon & Carriage Works Company Limited as it had diversified and now built almost everything from wheelbarrows to railway carriages. Its principal railway products were exported, though it constructed coach bodies for Great Northern Railway, GWR and Taff Vale Railway steam railmotors, some of the power units being supplied by the Avonside Engine Company. It also built some electric tramcars for the Bristol Tramways & Carriage Company. In 1920 Avonside was taken over by the Leeds Forge Company Limited and then the combined firms were absorbed by Cammell, Laird & Company which closed the Bristol works, rendering the 300 workers redundant. In 1924 the 13-acre site was purchased by the Bristol Tramways & Carriage Company for use as a bus and coach depot, while additionally, a central repair works was established later.

6

GOODS IN TRANSIT – COAL, BANANAS AND WAGONS OF WIND

Until the 1950s, railways were the country's main goods carrier: coal, raw materials and finished products, farm and market garden produce, fertilisers, items for sale in shops, all travelled by rail and a considerable proportion was carried to and from the railhead by road in railway vans and lorries.

Coal was vitally important, being used for domestic heating and cooking, industrial power and fuel for locomotives. Its use decreased in the 1960s when central heating by oil, electricity or gas became the norm. Practically all stations in the area had a coal yard and at least one coal merchant on site. To avoid paying demurrage charges (charges imposed by the railway after a certain number of days if a wagon/van was not unloaded), the coal was shovelled out of wagons into bunkers containing various grades and then, as required, shovelled into one-hundredweight sacks. Unscrupulous merchants sometimes watered dry coal to make it heavier!

For consignments of less than a wagon load, goods sheds performed functions very similar to those carried out in marshalling yards for individual wagons.

Just as a marshalling yard collected wagons to be formed into trains, so a goods shed collected small consignments into wagon loads.

Goods sheds dealt with a wide variety of consignments. A considerable proportion of their traffic was comparatively small packages to shops. These were easy to handle, barrow and stow, but there was always a proportion of articles of odd shapes, sizes and weights, so that the possibility of introducing mechanical appliances into a goods shed was limited.

Most goods sheds dealt with both forwarded and received traffic. Fortunately, pressure of work was eased by the fact that generally the pressure of received traffic fell in the earlier part of the day and that of forwarded traffic later in the day. Forwarded traffic was generally simpler: consignments brought in, often by railway lorry, either motor or horse, were barrowed to a suitable wagon. Received traffic could not always be barrowed to onwards transport, so a certain amount of dumping was required and this soon caused difficulty where accommodation was restricted. The provision of wide roadways was important to prevent traffic becoming blocked.

Cranes were required for lifting the occasional heavy article so even small goods yards or sheds often had one. These were manually operated since the cost of using a power-driven one was seldom warranted. Cranes were often fixed, but travelling road cranes were useful, particularly when some distance separated wagons from a road vehicle. Many stations were provided with an end loading dock, to enable a wheeled road vehicle to run on or off a railway wagon, thus obviating the need for lifting.

Until the 1950s, railways used horses for local delivery, these animals proving cheaper for distances for about up to a mile. In the 1930s the LMS calculated:

Cost of Delivery

Destination	Single horse	2 ton lorry	4 ton lorry	6 ton mechanical horse
¼ mile from station	10d	1s 5d	1s 9d	1s 0¼ d
½ mile from station	11¾d	1s 6d	1s 10d	1s 1d
1 mile from station	1s 3¼d	1s 8d	1s 11d	1s 2½d
1½ miles from station	1s 6½d	1s 10d	2s 1¾d	1s 3¾d

The use of containers, brought in during the 1930s, meant that goods did not have to be distributed in transit between senders' and receivers' premises. The cost of packing cases was saved, and also the cost of returning those empty packing cases.

The Canon's Marsh branch line gave direct access to a gasworks, a marble and slate importer, Fry's chocolate factory and Rowe Brothers' pipe and sheet lead works. Cattle could be discharged direct from ship to cattle trucks and spared being driven on the hoof through the city for a mile or two. Many of these cattle steamers arrived from Cork and Waterford. Cattle traffic always gave staff considerable work as the trucks required disinfecting with white bleach after use and pens had to be hosed down. As the ground was soft, Canon's Marsh goods shed was built on 274 ferro-concrete piles averaging 32 ft in depth. The building measured 540 ft by 133 ft and was equipped with eight electric cranes and three 30 cwt electric hoists. Its upper storey formed a warehouse.

The first GWR goods yard at Temple Meads was situated awkwardly at right angles to the passenger terminus and 12 ft below it on ground level. Access was by turntables and two hydraulic lifts acting rather like a pair of scales, simultaneously lowering one wagon while raising another, the operation taking about half a minute. The goods shed, measuring 326 ft by 138 ft, was equipped with cranes for loading and unloading wagons, of which the depot could hold 209. The wagon movements were by horse power and hydraulic capstans. Brunel wrote: 'We have several small capstan heads in different parts of the

The extensive Canon's Marsh goods depot in 1923, with Bristol Cathedral beyond.
(M.J. Tozer collection)

John Lysaght's advertisement of 1935, illustrating the GWR goods shed at Temple Meads, at that time the largest goods station in the world.

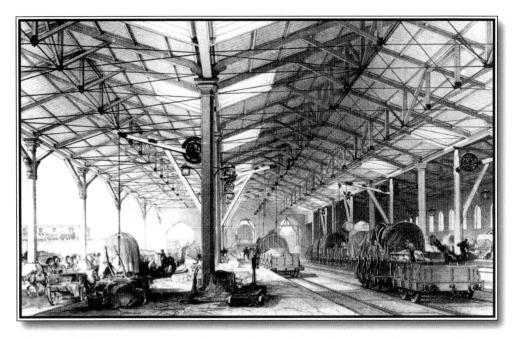

The first GWR goods station at Temple Meads. Notice the wagon lift, centre distance, and beyond the passenger lines, left, at a higher level. To the right of the nearest pillar is a portable weighing machine used for checking weights of items in transit – some senders were known to have under-declared weights when checked against the accompanying invoice. (J.C. Bourne)

station, which are always in motion running round and a porter takes a turn round one of these with a rope which is hooked on to any carriage which he wishes to move.' This GWR shed also handled B&E traffic until 1850 when its own shed opened at Pylle Hill.

The original GWR goods depot was soon unable to cope with the expanding traffic and so was rebuilt between 1874 and 1876. The old barge dock was filled in and replaced with a new wharf with steam and hydraulic cranes. The goods yard was raised 3½ feet and the layout rearranged to offer six platforms averaging 445 ft in length. As inwards traffic was less than outwards, only Platform No 1 was used for this traffic and also No 2 until 9 am. The wagons received on these two inwards roads, when empty, could be moved round to the outwards roads by capstan and horses. Access was down a gradient of 1 in 60 which assisted shunting. By 1914, approximately 1,700 wagons used the depot daily.

A further expansion in 1924, when surrounding property was purchased, created a new depot covering more than five acres, 15 platforms being under one roof. Each pair of platforms was connected to those adjacent by means of tip-up balance bridges to facilitate trolleying, and electric capstans were provided to move wagons. An electric telpher (an overhead travelling electric hoist) conveyed goods up to a weight of one ton to any part of the shed, and goods were also conveyed on electric platform trucks. Electric lifts serviced the cellarage for storing perishables such as butter, cheese, lard and bacon.

Many lineside firms had their own siding, such as Messrs John Lysaght Ltd's steel works at Bristol. Then there were Crown Brickyard, ICI and Commonwealth Smelting Ltd at Avonmouth, while oil tankers were also dealt with at that port.

From March 1901 when the first consignment of bananas arrived at Avonmouth, this traffic was highly important. In the week before the arrival of two banana boats, 700 vans were required to be strawed, weighed empty, steam heated to 68°F and eventually weighed full. Wagons of loose straw, known to railwaymen as 'wagons of wind', arrived from local stations. The Port of Bristol Authority (PBA) owned a fleet of steam, and later diesel, locomotives to work traffic within the dock area. Portishead also had a smaller stud of PBA engines.

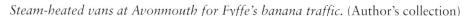

Steam-heated vans at Avonmouth for Fyffe's banana traffic. (Author's collection)

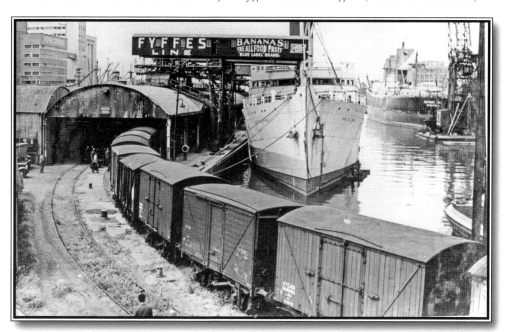

PBA 0-6-0ST No S8 Westbury *at Avonmouth, April 1964. It was built at Bristol by Messrs Peckett in 1934.* (W.F. Grainger)

Fry's 0-4-0T Sentinel shunter at Somerdale, Keynsham. It has a vertical boiler within the cab. This locomotive is now awaiting restoration at the Avon Valley Railway at Bitton. (M.J. Tozer collection)

With the opening of Fry's new factory at Keynsham in 1925, a siding was provided to the works and wagons moved within the confines by its own locomotive. Inwards traffic was sacks of cocoa beans, sugar and coal. Outwards came chocolate products in vans, labelled 'Return to J.S. Fry & Sons siding, Keynsham & Somerdale, GWR'. The vans which brought the raw materials were used to despatch the finished product. Fry's had depots in various parts of the country from which chocolate was delivered to the shops by road – often in railway-owned and operated vans, but wearing Fry's livery.

Also at Keynsham was a siding serving a paper mill – pulp and coal arriving and paper despatched. Steel bars arrived on bogie bolsters for the Square Grip Reinforcement Company. Tate & Lyle's also had a siding, but it saw little use. On the GWR at Bath, Stanley Engineering Co had a siding, while Stothert & Pitt, crane manufacturers, used the GWR's Westmoreland goods yard.

Quite a few industrial concerns in the area had their own locomotive, or fleet of locomotives. The PBA had the most extensive, mostly working at Avonmouth, but with a few at Portishead. The South West Gas Board had locomotives at Canon's Marsh, Bristol; Stapleton Road, Bristol and Bath gas works. Other users were Albright & Wilson, chemical works, Portishead;

Trade card: 15 of Davey & Co Ltd's pantechnicons loaded on railway wagons at Clifton Down station, c.1900. A GWR 0-6-0 heads the train. (Peter G. Davey)

Trade card: two MR horse-drawn lorries convey cartons of Chivers' carpet soap from the factory at Bath to the goods shed. (M.J. Tozer collection)

Coalpit Heath Colliery, its mile-long route from Westerleigh Sidings being the remains of the Bristol & Gloucestershire Railway; the East Bristol Colliery, Kingswood; the Imperial Smelting Co Limited, Avonmouth, which had standard gauge and 2 ft gauge steam locomotives; John Lysaght Limited's steel works, Feeder Road, Bristol; and Peckett & Sons Limited – the colliery locomotive shunted the works until the pit closed in April 1936, after which Messrs Peckett used *Nancy*, Peckett No 1067 of 1905, until scrapped in 1958.

An advantage of driving an industrial, rather than a main line engine was that you worked regular hours instead of clocking on at various times. One Pines Express driver had stomach ulcers and required set mealtimes. In order that he could enjoy regular meals, he gave up working for BR and changed to driving the Bath gas works engine. Quite a contrast.

Until 1858 the Midland Railway shared the GWR's goods depot at Temple Meads, but that year the MR inwards goods department moved to the company's coal yard at St Philip's, where a goods shed was erected. In 1866 it was doubled in size in order to accommodate the outwards goods department. The building measured 180 ft by 133 ft and its equipment included fifteen 2-ton

Westerleigh Sidings, view Up, 21 April 1960. The wagon repair depot can be seen on the far left. (Author)

hydraulic cranes, six hydraulically-powered traversing tables and hydraulic capstans. Spacious cellarage permitted the storage of over 15,000 hogsheads of ales consigned to tradesmen in the area. The building also stabled 50 MR horses. In due course, electric cranes supplanted those of the hydraulic pattern.

Beside the Floating Harbour – so-called because ships could load at any state of the tide – was Avonside Wharf, with a covered dock where traffic could be transferred from barge to wagon quite protected from the weather. The MR had its own fleet of barges for transferring goods to and from vessels and also the MR's King's Wharf depot, not rail-served, which formed waterside premises near St Mary's Redcliffe church.

In addition to dealing with general traffic, occasionally a new locomotive was despatched by Peckett's from their private siding. Prior to its acceptance by BR, its wheels had to be checked to ensure they were the correct gauge. Dead engines weighing less than 30 tons were required to be marshalled next to the rear brake van.

Although Mangotsfield was the junction of the Bristol & Gloucester line with the Bath branch, and was important for passenger exchange, it dealt with

The MR's King's Wharf depot, June 1898; it was not served by rail. The spire of St Mary's Redcliffe church is beyond. (Author's collection)

very little goods traffic, the exception being the private siding to Carson's chocolate factory. Crews shunting this siding had the concession of being allowed to purchase sweetmeats at a reduced rate.

Warmley, though having only three goods roads, dealt with a variety of traffic. Apart from general merchandise, it received the products from an adjacent brick and pipe works. About five wagons of ochre were despatched daily, mostly red, but also black, blue, green and yellow. It was interesting for porters' wives to see what colour their husbands would be when they arrived home. On alternate days a lorry arrived with a consignment of Douglas motor cycles.

One day when a Bath to St Philip's stopping passenger train drew up at Warmley, a man with a dead hen under his arm asked the driver if it was the train to Bristol. He was given an answer in the affirmative and invited onto the footplate. The train set off and in conversation it transpired that he owned a poultry farm and was taking the bird for an autopsy. Believing that one good turn deserves another, this farmer turned up at Warmley station a few days later with five sacks of hens' manure for the driver's allotment. For the rest of his duty that day the driver had to contend with the stench on the footplate. On arrival at Bath he secured a porter's trolley to wheel it to his garden.

Bitton's specialities included material going to and from a paper mill, machinery, steel sheets, hides, and chemicals. Moulding sand was despatched for Sheffield, with an insistence that the wagon must be absolutely clean thus ensuring that the load would not be contaminated. Mushrooms, flowers and other market garden produce were also despatched.

On the outskirts of Bath a malt-house was built on land purchased from the MR. It had its own siding, which locomotives were banned from entering. A capstan was provided, but as this was not always operational and moving the heavy wire cable was laborious, staff often preferred to move wagons by means of a pinch bar. Nearby was a siding to a cement works, later replaced by a timber yard. On 7 October 1919 the wood ignited and the conflagration delayed the 1.25 pm Bath to St Philip's passenger train for an hour and a half. When the train was eventually allowed to proceed, it was soaked with water to prevent the coachwork paint blistering. Jets of water were played on the sleepers and also the Up advanced starting signal to prevent them burning.

The principal traffic at Weston (Bath) station was coal, Charles Jobbins, stationmaster for 27 years, also being the coal merchant.

Class 5 4-6-0 No 44944 approaches Mangotsfield with a Down express. Carson's chocolate factory can be seen in the background. This water column was the only one between Westerleigh and Bristol. (Colin Roberts)

The MR had two goods yards at Bath. At the Junction Yard, near the junction with the Somerset & Dorset Railway (S&D), an arriving train would have to be reversed into No 1 Road and then shunted. Roads 2 and 3 were used to form trains for Templecombe and Bournemouth, while No 4 Road was for Bath transfers such as general merchandise for the goods shed, coal for the merchants, or timber for Hill's siding. No 5 Road held 'short traffic', that is, wagons which were only travelling a few miles down the S&D.

Bath gas works was the principal trader, 40 loaded wagons arriving daily and amounting to 3,200 tons of coal weekly. When snow thawed and then refroze, forming an ice block in a wagon, it was the practice to place a tray of burning coke beneath it.

The second yard at Bath was the Midland Bridge Road goods depot which was extensive and had a goods shed. Near the engine shed was the Boat Road, giving access to a wharf whose roof covered railway wagons and barges. At Bath the MR had a fleet of at least five barges carrying goods to such places as Bradford-upon-Avon and Trowbridge on the Kennet and Avon Canal. A maximum of 2½ tons of rags were taken to Bradford-upon-Avon, the barge returning with rubber or flock. As traffic was slight, three narrow boats were purchased as these were cheaper to operate. Paper for the *Wiltshire Times* arrived from Bath by canal and was transported onwards to the printers by an MR Straker steam lorry, built at Fishponds, Bristol. The MR waterway service from Bath ceased on 31 May 1912.

From the Boat Road a siding led to Stothert & Pitt's Victoria Works, wagons on Stothert's tracks being moved by adapted Fordson tractors. As most of its products, chiefly cranes, were carried on bogie vehicles, or long-wheelbase four-wheelers, derailments sometimes occurred on the twisting road.

The S&D had two sidings off its line at Oldfield Park. Half a mile from Bath Junction, May's siding opened on 8 April 1890 to serve a brickworks – traffic was mainly inwards coal, as bricks usually left by road. Railwaymen worked allotments beside the line and one S&D guard had land near the brickworks, from where he laboriously collected water to store in a tank. Suspecting a neighbour of stealing his precious liquid, he fed weed killer into the tank. Shortly afterwards, he observed that his neighbour's row of beans had died. When the brickworks closed in September 1939, this source of water was denied him and he was forced to beg a supply from drivers of returning banking engines. As a banker was only allowed 14 minutes to come out from Bath Junction and go back, the transfer of water had to be carried out smartly.

Three quarters of a mile from Bath Junction, the Bath & Twerton Co-op siding opened in 1911. Principal traffic was coal for household use and for the adjacent Co-op bakery, also flour and salt. In order to avoid making a special trip, vehicles for this siding were placed in front of a banking engine, the vehicles not being coupled to the train's brake van.

Apart from the goods depots already mentioned, there were depots in the area for sorting wagons. Due to the space required for these yards, they were situated on the edges of Bristol. The GWR had East Depot, West Depot and later Stoke Gifford. Similarly the LMS had Westerleigh Sidings.

East Depot opened in 1890 to cope with the extra traffic which developed in the area following the opening of the Severn Tunnel. The Up sidings were converted to the more economical hump working on 7 October 1923, this gravity method saving the cost of about 100 engine hours weekly. To enable the shunter in charge of the ground frame to communicate with the shunting engine driver, a Klaxon horn was installed. One blast indicated 'Go ahead', two 'Come back', three 'Stop' and six 'Obstruction'.

On the other side of the city, West Depot opened in 1906, while Stoke Gifford had been opened in 1903, conjointly with the opening of the Badminton cut-off. Stoke Gifford yard was intended to cope mainly with Avonmouth traffic, and closed on 4 October 1971; most of its site was used for Bristol Parkway station and the adjoining car park.

Stoke Gifford Yard, view Down, c. 1930. (Author's collection)

STATIONS AND SIGNALS

Successful use of the platform space of a railway station required much skill. Passenger platforms were generally of three kinds: those at the side of a track, an island platform, or a bay platform.

Island platforms were particularly useful at junctions where it was possible for a passenger changing trains merely to step across the platform from one train to another, rather than having to use a subway or footbridge – a financial advantage to the railway was that fewer platform staff were required. Bay platforms made for compactness in a station layout, but were only suitable for relatively infrequent services, taking up considerable terminal time. In steam days they were expensive in engine power, too, unless an engine release road was provided and this involved yielding a considerable amount of valuable space, although push and pull working, whereby the engine stayed at the same end of the train, avoided the need for running round.

Platform occupation plans had to be drawn up for busy times of the day, and consideration given to the desirability of trains for the same destinations leaving from the same platform, particularly if running a regular interval service. Connecting trains, especially where the margin was small, were, if possible, platformed in convenient relation to each other. Convenience for engine working was another vitally important matter.

The installation of public address systems at larger stations in the area was a boon to both passengers and staff. Almost incessant interrogation of staff by passengers was very wearing and few could stand up to it without occasional signs of irritation. Yet, to ensure that passengers continued to use the railway, their trip needed to be as pleasant an experience as possible. A wise stationmaster trained his staff to maintain a cheerful and courteous attitude towards his passengers.

*Stationmaster Joseph Cornelius Chidgey with his staff at Redland c.1905.
Their caps bear the insignia 'CER'. (M.J. Tozer collection)*

Temple Meads had a Superintendent rather than a stationmaster, the Superintendent being only responsible for operation and the fabric of the buildings. Other duties undertaken by normal stationmasters were covered by independent men: Guard's Inspector, Parcel Agent and Passenger Manager.

The post of Superintendent was filled alternately by a man from the GWR and the LMS. For example, W. Orton (LMS) was succeeded by W. Thick (GWR). When a new platform timetable was to be issued, to save the task of writing everything out, necessary alterations were made to an old timetable which was then sent to the printer. The first time this was done following Thick's appointment, one of the clerk's amendments was to delete 'Orton' and replace it with 'Thick'. When the proofs were returned by the printer, the clerk was surprised to discover that 'Orton' had been printed in bold, wide letters!

With the opening of the B&E, Brunel's original terminus at Temple Meads proved somewhat unsatisfactory because through trains required backing into or out of the station. In 1845 a simple terminus was erected for B&E trains originating or finishing at Bristol and for the remainder, a curved platform was provided on the through line to the GWR. In view of the proximity of the cattle market and also its relatively primitive construction, the B&E station was popularly known as 'The Cow Shed'.

By the 1860s, Temple Meads had become inadequate for the volume of GWR, B&E and MR traffic, so in 1871 work was begun on an enlargement and a new thoroughfare, Victoria Street/Temple Street, which created a better link with the city centre. The B&E station was demolished and a curved train shed with a span of 125 ft erected on its site. Brunel's original train shed was lengthened in a style matching the original, but with metal, and not timber, roof supports. The new station, designed by Sir Matthew Digby Wyatt, aided by Francis Fox of the B&E, opened on 1 January 1878. It had an approach road rising to a very pleasing entrance at platform level, rather than at ground level as had previously been the case. Each of the three companies had its own booking office within the Great Hall and passengers entered by one of three labelled doors – one for each company.

Even before the enlargement was completed, it was realised that the station facilities would still be inadequate, but the abolition of the broad gauge in 1892 enabled an additional island platform to be fitted in, which slightly eased the situation.

By the 1920s, traffic had grown to such proportions that on bank holidays, trains were held in block from Highbridge waiting for a platform at Temple Meads and even then having to wait outside the station for an hour. On at least one occasion, the time taken to run the last mile into Temple Meads was three hours twenty minutes! In 1929, as a measure to help alleviate the Depression, the government offered loans to carry out large public works and the enlargement of Temple Meads qualified. A large portion of the adjoining cattle market was purchased and, under the direction of P. E. Culverhouse, the station was doubled in size, the work being completed in December 1935. Surprisingly, gas lights were used for the new platforms and remained in use until 1960 when they were replaced by florescent tubes. All the main platforms had refreshment and waiting rooms.

Signalling is vital to efficient railway working. In 1909 Temple Meads was controlled by four mechanical boxes, two of which each contained 105 levers. When the station was extended in 1935, mechanical signalling was replaced by three power boxes.

Temple Meads East was the largest signal box on the GWR and replaced two mechanical boxes. It had 23 block bells, each with a different tone and the box was in communication with no fewer than seven adjacent boxes. It was of three-storey design, whereas the similar West and Locomotive boxes were only two storeys. Points were shifted electrically and signals were coloured lights. The East box had 368 'levers', which were actually slides drawn to a halfway position where they locked until the point or light had actually functioned

4-6-0 No 5927 Guild Hall *at Temple Meads with a twelve-coach Birkenhead to Paignton train, 4 August 1934. It is using one of the new platforms. Signalling is still mechanical.* (E.J.M. Hayward)

correctly, when they could then be pulled out to their fullest extent. Three special class signalmen and a booking boy were always on duty. The West box had 328 levers, 20 bells and was also worked by three men and a booking boy.

Bristol Parkway station opened on 1 May 1972, on the site of the redundant marshalling yard (see Chapter 6). It proved a great success as it provided plenty of free parking. Car-owning passengers from Bath, if travelling north, found it more convenient to drive to Parkway, rather

Clifton Down station, view towards Avonmouth c.1960. (Lens of Sutton)

than board a train at Bath and then have to change at Temple Meads.

Clifton Down station was the most imposing Bristol suburban station, having a superb mansion-like booking hall with a huge fireplace at each end.

The north frontage of the GWR station at Bath faced the city and is the most attractive, that on the river side being plainer in style. Towards the end of the 19th century, Bath citizens were complaining about the dilapidated state of the station; in fact it was so bad that when Princess Helen visited Bath on 13 June 1889, instead of using the terrible structure, her train drew in to a special platform built just for her in the attractive Sydney Gardens. On 2 April 1889 the town clerk had submitted a petition, signed by 11,000 citizens, to the GWR directors, asking for station improvements. Although a wide staircase to the Up platform was in place, it was kept closed, forcing passengers to use the alternative, the exit of which was only the width of a walking stick held sideways. Eventually, in 1893 the wide staircase was made available and two years later the station was lit by electricity – one of the first in the country to have this form of illumination.

In 1897 the train shed was removed, an Up bay platform created and the main platforms widened and extended as far as possible without blocking access to the stub sidings at the end of both platforms. Wagons could be detached, or attached to trains using a shunting horse. The animal was hooked to the side of a van, gave a strong pull and stepped aside, the impetus fly-shunting the van to

Princess Helen arriving at Bath's Sydney Gardens, 13 June 1889. This station was erected specially for her as the citizens believed that the ordinary one was unworthy of royalty. Mixed gauge is in evidence. (Author's collection)

BR Standard class 5 4-6-0 No 73050 arrives at Bath Green Park from Bournemouth West. Notice the bonded stores on the right. (Dr Christopher Kent)

buffer up to a train standing at the platform. To ease the work of the horse, its keeper used a pinch bar behind a wheel to help set it in motion. Prince, the last shunting horse at the station, retired in 1959.

The Up platform had two refreshment rooms – one for first class and the other for all classes – but the Down platform had only one refreshment room. Recycling was practised in 1867 when a box to collect newspapers, magazines and books discarded by passengers was fixed to each of the platforms so that they could be given to patients of the Royal United and Mineral Water hospitals.

From 1845 until 26 January 1936 an unusual feature at the station was an open girder footbridge which offered a direct connection between the Up platform and the Royal Hotel on the opposite side of the street.

The Midland Railway station at Bath had a pseudo-Georgian frontal, with slender Ionic columns above the ground floor and a balustraded parapet concealing the roof, the whole being well-balanced by a delicate *porte-cochère*, all complementing the 66-ft-span train shed.

At the west end of the arrival platform, a bonded warehouse enabled vans to be shunted into the secure building where wines and spirits were lowered by a

2-4-0 No 104, still in Midland Railway livery, at Bath LMS station having run through the blocks, 13 February 1925.
(Author's collection)

three-ton crane into cellars extending the full length of the platforms, casks being carried on narrow gauge wagons.

Between 8 pm and 8.30 pm on Fridays, pigeon clubs set up tables on the platform, loading the baskets which were placed in vans, taken to Mangotsfield and added to a train from Bristol bound for the north. Porters disliked handling pigeon baskets because of the smell and the mess created by their occupants. Incoming pigeons were released from their baskets in the goods yard, which was open with no overhead wires.

Most terminal stations had at least one instance of a train running through the buffers and Bath was no exception. Early on the morning of 13 February 1925 a W.H. Smith & Sons newsboy was sitting on a seat with his back to the buffers. Hearing furious whistling from 2-4-0 No 104 approaching with a parcels train from the Midlands, he leaped up and sped away. This was most fortunate as No 104 demolished the buffers and an ornamental bank of ferns and mounted the platform, shattering the seat on which he had been sitting.

Packing was placed under the locomotive's wheels to prevent them from sinking through the timber floor into the bonded store below. Two other engines attempted but failed to pull No 104 back the 27 ft to the track. Its wheels were then jacked up and a third engine coupled on and thus it was brought back on to its proper road at 11.10 am. The newsboy's abandoned overcoat was found beneath the engine.

8

FRESH MILK AND STRAWBERRIES

Farmers felt the effects of the railway age from the beginning. When a line was being built, land had to be taken, often cutting farms in half. To enable farmers to cross the line, cattle creeps or bridges were constructed under or over the railway. Usually this arrangement was satisfactory, but in December 1874 James Kelson of Bath took the Somerset & Dorset to court.

Kelson owned a 28-acre market garden and dairy farm in the area of Bath now known as Oldfield Park. Prior to the S&D's construction, Kelson had a roadway from one end of his property to the other, but the railway had bisected this road and blocked it. He applied to the company to make a level crossing, but instead of carrying out the promised work, the railway built a platform for ticket inspection. Kelson insisted to the court that an accommodation bridge or level crossing should be made, that a bridge already existing on his property must be made larger and wider, and that a ditch be made sufficiently wide to carry water into a culvert. Finally, he wanted a watering place for his cattle to be made in one of the fields to replace one which had been cut off.

The S&D kindly provided a special train to convey the magistrates to the scene of the dispute. At the hearing the company contended that Kelson had been a difficult gentleman to satisfy. For the 1 acre 3 roods and 30 perches of his land which the railway required, he demanded £2,300. In order to save the expense of arbitration the S&D had offered £700 and undertook to make a level crossing. As Kelson had rejected this offer and opted for arbitration, the S&D said it was no longer liable to make that crossing (the arbitrator decided that his land was worth £926). James Kelson won the day and the Bench ordered that the works which the S&D had offered to make – to create a culvert and improve access to his market garden – be carried out.

A farm removal train at Bitton, September 1933. One wagon carries implements, while in front of the cattle wagon, left, is a container loaded with the household furniture. (Author's collection)

The arrival of railways in an area affected farming economically too. Hitherto many farmers had grown oats to feed stagecoach teams and other horses, but demand for this cereal fell overnight and farmers had to diversify. Many changed to dairying as fresh milk could be taken swiftly to cities, without the need to turn surplus milk into butter or cheese. Cattle could be transported by rail to large markets where a higher price could be obtained and would arrive in far better condition than if they had been driven on the hoof.

Pigs and sheep were other animals sent by rail, and also day-old chicks. New potatoes appeared in the area earlier than normal, being brought by rail from Cornwall, or by steamer and rail from the Channel Islands. Likewise strawberries were sent from the Cheddar Valley. Farmers' wives used the trains to take eggs to market. The railway would also bring fertilisers which the farmers often collected from the goods yard. Implement makers, having a wider market than in pre-railway days, could produce machinery on a larger scale, and thus cheaper.

Railways also enabled entire farms to be moved – people, furniture, animals and machinery – from one part of the country to another.

Although rail transport for cattle was generally very safe, accidents could happen. On 28 May 1912 the 12.20 pm Bath to Bournemouth passenger train had attached to it three vans containing seven bulls and six heifers, the property of Viscount Portman of Blandford. They had been exhibited at the Bath & West Show, held that year actually at Bath. The three prize animals travelled in a van which had a special compartment for the two herdsmen travelling with them.

As the train plodded up the gradient of 1 in 50 through Oldfield Park towards Devonshire Tunnel, the herdsmen heard the beasts stamping and could smell burning. They slid back the door between the two compartments and were met by a blast of smoke and flame. A cinder from the locomotive's chimney had set the straw bedding alight, the conflagration fanned by the draught caused by the train's movement. One of the cowmen had the presence of mind to pull the communication cord before both took a flying leap onto the track.

As the cattle wagon was by now a flaming furnace, any attempt to rescue the creatures was out of the question. They were silent; they had been suffocated. The blazing vehicle was uncoupled and a space of twelve yards left at each end of the cattle truck to prevent flames from spreading to the rest of the train. Railwaymen attempted to douse the flames with buckets of water obtained from the engine, but all to no avail. The charred remains of the beasts were buried in an adjoining field.

9

RACE DAYS AND FOOTBALL SPECIALS

Sports specials were often a worthwhile way of using idle locomotives and rolling stock. The Midland Railway/London, Midland & Scottish ran specials from the Midlands to Bath on race days. Some passengers got off at Kelston: although on the map it seemed like a relatively easy 2½-mile walk across fields from the station to the course, in reality it involved a climb of 700 ft. Usually just under half the passengers opted to walk from Kelston, the others travelling on to Bath and obtaining transport there. It is believed that the last race day special to Bath Green Park was on Thursday, 14 May 1959 when BR Standard class 5 4-6-0 No 73156, shedded at Derby, worked this York to Bath train.

On race days, the railway police were much in evidence at Kelston as bookies and punters tried to avoid paying fares, while after the races, welshing bookmakers hid in the bushes and then tried to leap into an Up train at the last possible minute.

Race trains ceased to use Kelston after about 1930, but the GWR continued to operate race specials to Bath, as did the Western Region of British Railways. Fleets of Bath Tramways buses carried passengers onwards to the course. In earlier times, some passengers got off at Saltford, crossed the river and walked up to the racecourse. On race days the ferryman borrowed a larger boat to make his task easier as he required fewer trips.

Other sports users of Kelston station were those attending Saltford Regatta, the MR/LMS issuing cheap tickets, as did the GWR, the latter running a special train when the first regatta was held in 1849. The Avon Rowing Club had a

Saltford, view Up. The Avon can be seen left of the GWR line, while the MR runs on the further bank. (Author's collection)

boathouse at Saltford and the GWR offered members the privilege of cheap return tickets. On regatta days additional trains called at Saltford, and in August 1872 the MR brought 1,200 passengers from Birmingham. On at least one occasion, a steam railmotor carried the Monkton Combe School crew and supporters from Monkton Combe, on the Camerton branch, to Saltford. One day an 'eight' was carried by rail from Monkton Combe to Saltford. Too long for one wagon, it was spread over two. Unfortunately, a keen porter secured it to both wagons, so you can imagine what happened at the first curve!

In December 1890 hundreds of people travelled to Saltford and Kelston stations to skate on a nearby sheet of ice. Latterly, however, since Kelston station was three-quarters of a mile from the village, over a footpath which was often muddy in winter, it received little traffic originating locally. Most of its passengers were anglers out for a day's fishing. As they had return tickets, Kelston receipts were usually less than a pound per month.

Bulleid Pacifics occasionally appeared at Bristol heading football specials from the Southern Region. West Country class No 34047 *Callington* and No 34048 *Crediton* worked such trains on 20 March 1954, and were probably the first of the class to visit the city. On 8 January 1955 no fewer than four Pacifics headed

Despite the caption on the picture, the running-in board reads: 'Ashton Gate Platform'. The steam railmotor is destined for Bath. (M.J. Tozer collection)

trains from Portsmouth to Stapleton Road, with supporters heading for Bristol Rovers' ground. On 13 November 1955 an excursion was run from Brighton to Weston-super-Mare via Salisbury as a West Country promotional exercise. It was worked throughout by 4-6-2 No 34090 *Sir Eustace Missenden, Southern Railway*.

Ashton Gate Platform, close to Bristol City's football ground, opened on 15 September 1906 to cater for football crowds, a special train being run direct from Clifton Down, but the station was not served by regular trains until 23 May 1926. Despite the general withdrawal of passenger trains from the branch on 7 September 1964, Ashton Gate still enjoyed intermittent use by football specials between 1970 and 1977.

10

TIME FOR A GOOD BOOK

It is not always realised that railways were an important factor in the spread of literacy. Companies encouraged their staff to learn to read and write, in an era when only about half the population could read or sign their name because, as running the systems grew more and more complicated, they were required to study rule books and complete various forms. It was partly this increased demand for literacy in railway operation and other developing industries that brought about the passing of the 1870 Education Act, which for the first time required that all children attend primary school.

Railways also brought about reading on the move. Crammed into a stagecoach, or perched in the wind and weather on its outside, was no place to read, but the space and smoothness of a first or second class railway coach offered the opportunity to read as a diversion, just as many today read while on a flight.

William Marshall recognised that some railway travellers would not wish to gaze out of the window continuously, or stare at their surroundings while waiting for a train. He had the brilliant idea that they should be entertained by literature, so in 1841 set up a bookstall at Fenchurch Street station, London. His enterprise prospered and others imitated his idea.

Railway companies were all in favour because they received payment for allowing a firm to set up bookstalls on their stations. In fact it was H.B. Marshall, son of the founder of the bookstall at Fenchurch Street, who held the contract for setting up bookstalls on GWR stations, while Walkey & Son held a similar contract for the Bristol & Exeter. In addition to reading material, H.B. Marshall was allowed to sell sandwiches, confectionery and bottled beer. Railway bookstalls often sold candle handlamps to supplement the poor compartment lighting. Sometimes the lamps sold had a pointed end which could be thrust into the upholstery to steady them.

A newspaper stall at the Bath MR station c.1903. (Author's collection)

Between 1863 and 1905 nearly all the thousand or so English and Welsh bookstalls were run by W.H. Smith. Good trade was done as the Victorians went regularly to their local station to purchase a newspaper, or change their subscription circulating library books. The library stock was exchanged by train with headquarters. When W.H. Smith lost the GWR contract in 1905 through the railway demanding a higher price than he thought reasonable, he reacted against this fall in trade by opening bookstalls in town high streets, sometimes just outside a station. In addition to catering for the travelling public, railway bookstalls also supplied books to people in the locality and treated them as valued customers, sometimes even delivering the books personally if there was no convenient carrier.

Until the coming of the railways, weekly local papers echoed news taken from those published in London. Thus, national news tended to be stale because, as mail coaches ran at night, a London paper did not even begin its journey until it was about twelve hours old. By 1845 W.H. Smith had increased circulation figures when he chartered nine special overnight trains to transport London papers to Bath, Bristol and other parts of England and Wales.

Running a railway bookstall in the 19th century was certainly no sinecure. It was not just a simple matter of selling the reading material – much hard work went on behind the scenes. Contemporary newspapers were delivered to the stalls in sheets which required folding and the pages put together. *The Times* consisted of three sheets and the *Daily Telegraph* two. Until the rival *Graphic* started which arrived folded and stitched, the *Illustrated London News* magazine was also required to be folded and the sheets placed in order.

Then, after folding, the papers and magazines had to be laid out attractively to catch the eye of potential customers. Trains sometimes caused problems; an express train speeding through Keynsham, for instance, would send the stock blowing about.

In 1878 W.H. Smith & Son suffered through its honesty. No enclosures of items such as books or magazines were allowed in parcels carried by rail at the cheap newspaper rate. Thus W.H. Smith paid for two parcels: newspapers in one and other reading matter in another. Other wholesalers ignored this stipulation. One morning railway staff cut the string on all newspaper parcels and found stationery, books and magazines packed in with the newspapers – but not in those consigned by W.H. Smith.

Not all literature sold on railway bookstalls was pure and wholesome and as W.H. Smith banned pornography from his stalls, he was nicknamed 'Old Morality'.

Although the novelist Anthony Trollope welcomed railway bookstalls, he was not impressed with the standard of literature offered – poor English novels, translations from the French and imports from the USA. This was perhaps an unjustified criticism for things were certainly improving and some publishers made the effort to produce cheap paper-covered editions of worthwhile books especially for the railway bookstall market.

In 1847 the publishers Simms & Macintyre issued their 'Parlour Library' at a shilling per volume. *The Times* criticised the venture, claiming that 'every addition to the stock was positively made on the assumption that persons of the better class who constitute the larger portion of railway readers lose their accustomed taste the moment they enter the station'. Nevertheless, so successful was it that in 1848 it spawned an imitation: Routledge's Railway Library. In 1851, the year of the Great Exhibition saw the start of no fewer than three similar series: Bentley's Railroad Library, Murray's Railway Reading and Longman's Travellers' Library. Not all these included novels, but Messrs Routledge continued publishing books in the series for 50 years and ended with a list of almost 1,300 titles. Other publishers issued guides, examples being *Bradshaw's Railway Companion*, J.C. Bourne's *The History & Description of the Great Western Railway*, George Measom's *The Official Illustrated Guide to the Great Western Railway* and his *Official Guide to the Bristol & Exeter Railway*.

Circa 1900 the format of books sold on stalls changed from large page paperbacks to pocket-size with cloth covers. Until the First World War the price remained at about 8d, a considerable reduction of price on a three-volume novel which at the beginning of the 1860s had cost £1 11s 6d – more than most working men earned in a week.

II

RAILWAYS AT WAR

THE FIRST WORLD WAR

Railways in the First World War played a vital role in transporting men and war supplies, including the horses and mules which then formed an important part of army transport. Almost 350,000 horses and mules were landed at Avonmouth and walked to the remount depot at Shirehampton, there to receive veterinary attention and be distributed in cattle trucks. Shirehampton dealt with up to 60 wagons a day – mostly containing hay or sawdust for the horses. About twelve wagons of manure were despatched daily, some destined for Cadbury Road station on the Weston, Clevedon & Portishead Light Railway.

Bristol, Avonmouth and Portishead grew in importance as Bristol Channel ports were safer than those on the English Channel, threatened by enemy attack from the sea and the air for the first time. Avonmouth Docks handled a vast amount of freight, in addition to the disembarkation and embarkation of 200,000 troops and also the war wounded from various eastern campaigns. Hospital trains left the Port of Bristol Authority's (PBA) dock station hauled by its own locomotives to Gloucester Road Crossing, but although the engines were fitted with vacuum brakes, in cold weather a GWR engine had to be brought in to provide steam to heat the stock. Avonmouth sent out over 130,000 wagon loads of guns, ammunition and stores to the fronts, particularly eastern ones. The first military tanks were said to have been despatched from Avonmouth, carefully hidden beneath sheeting to conceal this new secret weapon. Between 1914 and 1918, a total of some 3½ million tons, including civilian supplies, passed through.

Hallen Halt closed on 22 March 1915 as a wartime economy measure since there were so many other halts in the Bristol and Bath area, but was reopened

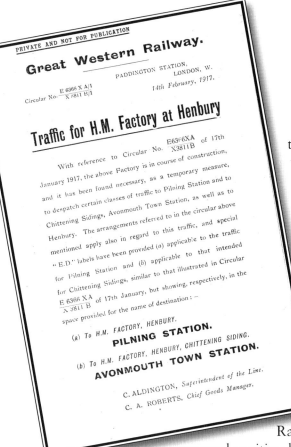

Notice dated 14 February 1917 regarding the construction of a munitions factory at Henbury. (M.J. Tozer collection)

to serve workers at a nearby war supplies factory. Chittening Platform was opened on 5 March 1917 for construction workers of what would have been the second largest government factory in the country but Armistice was declared before the factory was functional, while near St Andrew's Road a plant opened to produce sulphuric acid for munitions purposes.

Hotwells station, on the hitherto Bristol Port Railway & Pier line, was in a cramped position between river and cliff so when it was found essential to run trains of eight bogie coaches to carry workmen to Avonmouth, the only solution was to build a new station – Hotwells Extension Platform, a quarter of a mile downstream. As many as 2,000 men travelled to the old station at Hotwells by electric tram or on foot. Then, walking by the original station, they carried on past 'Point Villa' where refreshments were sold, to the new timber platform where they walked up a ramp to one of two ticket huts. The porter in the smaller hut only issued tickets to Avonmouth, while the stationmaster in the larger one offered a greater range of tickets. To save time, they date stamped the fourpenny workmen's returns from Hotwells to Avonmouth in any spare moments. The workmen also helped by trying to tender the correct fare.

After the morning rush, trains were shorter and could revert to using the original Hotwells station. Congestion was not so great in the evening either, as workmen's tickets were available for return to either Hotwells or Clifton Down.

This proved a great concession as many workmen could return to Clifton Down and then walk down to their homes, thus saving the tram fare.

On the Portishead branch, Portbury Shipyard station opened on16 September 1918 for the thousand Royal Engineers carrying out the construction. The shipyard was intended to replace vessels lost through enemy action, but due to the cessation of hostilities in November, it was never completed.

THE SECOND WORLD WAR

Avonmouth again was invaluable after the outbreak of war in September 1939. Between 1 and 4 September, 800 children in each of about a dozen trains, evacuated from south-east England, arrived in the area. And in the same year, it was used for the embarkation of troops and the shipment of supplies to the British Expeditionary Force in France and later on to the Mediterranean. Then, when the United States entered the war, a large proportion of its services' supplies, including locomotives, planes and tanks, were landed at Avonmouth.

Railways in the area suffered from air attacks such as that at Filton in November 1941 when the line from Avonmouth was severed. The yards at

0-6-0T No 1990 and 1999 built in the USA, being unloaded from SS Gleniffer at the Royal Edward Dock, Avonmouth, 24 March 1944. To speed unloading, they are placed in a lighter. (PBA)

Avonmouth held ammunition and oil trains, neither of which were pleasant to be near in an air raid. On hearing the siren warning, one GWR goods guard went to the footplate of the engine of his train. The fireman closed the firebox door so that no telltale light could be seen by enemy planes and, knowing that the firebox would act like armour plating on one side, set to work to build a wall of coal to provide protection from shrapnel and flying debris on the other. Other railwaymen were known to have taken shelter under vans during a raid, only to discover afterwards that those vans contained ammunition.

LMS driver Ted Smith experienced an air raid at Avonmouth. When incendiary bombs started to fall he sheltered under the tender with his young fireman. Then, during a lull they ran across to an air raid shelter. Already in there were two sets of GWR men, who later went out and were killed. Hearing the 'All Clear', Ted and his fireman went to a public house, but the German raiders returned, forcing the railwaymen to go back to the shelter. In this second raid a bomb destroyed a shunting engine and signal box, the signalman fortunately safe in his shelter. Following the next 'All Clear', Ted and his mate doused wagon fires with buckets of water.

TRAVELLING IN THE BLACKOUT

Throughout the war stations had reduced lighting and coaches were fitted with low-intensity lamps and had to have their blinds pulled down so only a dim light was emitted when a coach door was opened. Corridor windows were not blacked out, but a blue light was used. Netting was stuck on the windows to prevent the blast from exploding bombs shattering windows and sending sharp pieces of glass to lacerate flesh. Unfortunately it was a great temptation to boys to try and pick the netting off the glass.

Locomotives were a problem to black out. Those with side-window cabs had these plated over and sheets were supplied to fix between tender and roof in an attempt to hide the glow from open firebox doors. Engines could not be completely blacked out and Bristolians were concerned that light from locomotives could be seen by raiders. One night the RAF flew over Bristol to determine if railway lights could be spotted by enemy aircraft. It reported: 'Intense observation from the air did not reveal any lighting due to railway operations.'

The locomotive blackout sheets were secured in place by thick rubber bands. One night when his driver closed the regulator, Fireman Bob Ford turned on the blower to prevent a back draught causing the flames in the firebox to blow back into the cab. Unfortunately, the fire doors rattled apart and flame roared out. To escape the heat, the driver climbed out one side and Bob the other. The next thing they knew was that the blackout sheet stretching from cab to tender was alight. The driver reached in to apply the brake – it was conveniently placed for just such an emergency. Bob released the rubber bands from the four hooks on his side and the driver did the same for those on his side, allowing the blazing sheet to fly away into the night.

The passenger platforms at Bath were relatively short, only holding eight coaches, thus requiring the 16-coach wartime trains to draw up twice. During the blackout a sailor travelling in a coach towards the rear stepped out onto what he assumed was the platform. He took a further stride and plunged into the River Avon, where he was dragged down by the weight of his kit. Actually, he had stepped out on to a bridge parapet. Fortunately, this mishap did not have a fatal ending, but, heeding the warning and to prevent a repetition, the GWR erected a fence on the parapet.

Wartime travel was often so traumatic that many passengers vowed that when peace came, they would never travel by rail again. I vividly remember travelling to Newton Abbot from Bath when there were 16 passengers and a baby in my compartment which was designed for seating only eight. The corridor outside was jam-packed with people either standing, or sitting on cases.

Work in goods yards could not proceed with very dim lighting and busy yards were re-wired so that when enemy raiders were detected approaching, a switch could be thrown to reduce the lights. Even so, the amount of goods traffic which could be handled at night in the blackout, was reduced by a third.

Air raid alerts were given verbally to train crews by signalmen who stopped trains for this purpose:

'Yellow alert' – raiders had crossed the coast
'Purple alert' – warning of possible raid: shut firebox doors and erect blackout sheets
'Red alert' – raiders overhead

During a red alert, trains descending a gradient would proceed extremely slowly to avoid a glow from their brake blocks. In December 1939 the maximum permitted speed at any time was reduced to 50 mph, though during air raid alerts, speed was not allowed to exceed 25 mph in daylight and 15 mph at night – this being a precaution against trains falling into bomb craters, or gaps left by fallen bridges. At 15 mph it was difficult for a goods guard to keep the wagons 'off the engine' and even more difficult if the wagons had oil, rather than grease axle boxes since they ran more freely.

Gas attacks were expected and yellow gas-detecting paint applied to a level of six inches on the window of a locomotive's cab. Passengers carried gas masks, while footplate crews and guards were issued with service gas masks and steel helmets.

Temple Meads was a prime German target and was raided several times. On 6 December 1940 as the 7.10 pm to Salisbury left, it received a direct hit resulting in the deaths of the driver and 15 passengers. On the same day a bomb struck the east end of Bristol No 2 Tunnel and ricocheted into a coach; some of the rubble from bombing was taken to North Pier, Avonmouth, to reclaim land for future development. On 9 October 1941 a Whirlwind fighter aircraft crashed into the weighbridge pit at Saltford goods yard, killing the pilot.

In the Baedeker raids on Bath of 25/26 April 1942, 100 ft of Twerton Viaduct was demolished. The Down line had to be supported on temporary timbers and reopened on 28 April, but restoration of the Up line took longer. To cater for traffic in both directions, a temporary crossover was inserted between the tracks on each side of the breach so that, for a short distance, Up traffic could work over the Down line. Meanwhile, a temporary bridge was constructed to carry the Up line across the missing section of the viaduct. This was first used on 15 May.

Coaches damaged in a raid on Dr Day's Carriage Sidings, 24 November 1940. The view is towards Temple Meads. (Author's collection)

The east end of the Down platform of Bath GWR station following a raid, 26 April 1942. (Author's collection)

During these raids the foreman of the LMS shed at Bath had had the foresight to disperse engines to various parts of the goods yard, so that if the engine shed had received a direct hit, all would not be lost. When a raid was imminent, a plane spotter was stationed on top of the water softener to ring a bell to warn of the approach of hostile aircraft.

Two sets of coaches used for S&D services were normally kept overnight at Bath LMS station, but during the war they were taken to Bitton each evening for storage so that if the river bridge immediately outside the station had been bombed, the coaches would not have been trapped.

One evening as the last train of the day stood at Kelston station, a German plane dropped a flare. The terrified guard, expecting to be bombed or machine-gunned, quickly waved the train off. This was a pity, because the porter, who normally caught it, had to walk back along the track to his home in Bath.

Following the Normandy invasion, ambulance trains ferried the wounded between the ships and various hospitals. They were often headed by LNER class B12/3 4-6-0s because these engines were equipped with Westinghouse brakes (which many ambulance cars had) and were light enough to travel over most lines in Britain.

An ambulance train at Avonmouth Docks, 1944. (PBA)

ON THE RATION

When not working, fire-watching, or on Home Guard duty, railwaymen were likely to be found working on a lineside allotment growing food to eke out the rations. Particularly around the time of the Normandy landings, the S&D proved a vital link to the south coast, both for servicemen and their supplies. Special trains carried United States' troops from Liverpool Docks to the south coast for embarkation. After leaving Bath, hundreds of pre-packed meals were distributed throughout the train by trolleys. The greaseproof cardboard boxes contained coffee, dried milk, sugar, half a loaf, butter, tinned meat, sweets and chocolate. On arrival, the fireman took a sack and went through the train collecting unused food – a wonderful gleaning in those days of severe rationing. Such supplies were shared with other staff at Bath.

US troops sometimes gave railwaymen a headache. There was one occasion when a double-headed troop train stopped on the S&D at Midford because the communication cord had been pulled and thus the brakes had been applied. It was discovered that some of the servicemen had tied their kit bags to the communication cord. When the young fireman politely asked them to remove their bags, he was pelted with chewing gum. The train proceeded to the Midford advanced starting signal and then, because the cord had been pulled, it stopped again. The guard explained the problem to the commanding officer who failed to appreciate the difficulties his troops were causing. The delays were so great that the train arrived at Templecombe an hour and a half late.

Food rationing occasionally encouraged railwaymen to carry out less than honest actions. One goods guard was working a train from Taunton to Westbury via Bristol. At Bridgwater, the driver walked back to the guard and said that if the train stopped near Parson Street station he should take no notice. Sure enough, the train did stop there. Looking out, the guard saw the driver opening the doors of the station truck which, as usual, was immediately behind the engine. He took out a round cheese and rolled it down the embankment to the house where he lived, or rather that was his intention. Unfortunately for him, on the embankment was an anthill, this causing the cheese to jump into a neighbour's greenhouse. To calm the neighbour, he had to share the cheese.

A parallel experience happened to one my great-uncles. The bottom of one retired S&D driver's garden abutted the railway. To alleviate a coal shortage, one of his former colleagues positioned some sleeper off-cuts on the footplate and as he approached the retired driver's home, nudged them off. In theory they should have rolled down the embankment, pinged through the wire fence and ended in his garden. Unfortunately, he did not get the correct trajectory and one of them rolled down the embankment, pinged through the fence, but into my great-uncle's garden, where it punched a hole in his chicken house. My sagacious uncle, realising what had happened, asked his neighbour to make good the damage.

Although most railwaymen were patriotic, occasionally a rotten apple turned up in the barrel. On one occasion at Canon's Marsh Sidings, shunters deliberately allowed a van containing sugar to run hard against the stop block so that something on the van would break. They then placed a 'Not to Go' label on the wagon and put it in the cripples' siding where they were able to have longer to sample its contents.

A RESERVED OCCUPATION

In addition to their regular work, some railwaymen were on a fire-watching rota, so that when incendiary bombs fell they could either be removed with a shovel, or the flames doused with a stirrup pump, or if the fire grew out of hand, the fire brigade could be called. Other railway staff joined the Local Defence Volunteers (later to become the Home Guard) and, in their spare time, patrolled goods yards, bridges and tunnels in the Bristol/Bath area to guard against attack by German saboteurs or paratroops. One enthusiastic Home Guard patrolling Bath LMS goods yard shot at a railway guard who failed to identify himself when challenged. Fortunately the bullet missed.

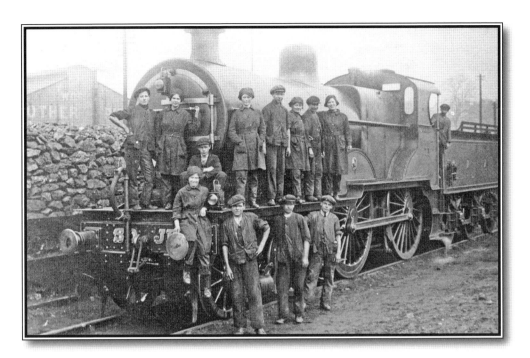

Male and female engine cleaners stand on S&D 4-4-0 No 71 at Bath during the First World War. (Author's collection)

The job of railwayman was classed as a 'reserved occupation' and thus the men were exempt from conscription into the forces, but many railwaymen did enlist. LMS Driver Doug Holden from Bath was conscripted and was sent to the Longmoor Military Railway in Hampshire. He was intended to be sent to India, but as it was discovered that railways in Britain were becoming short of skilled manpower, shortly before he was to leave an officer called out, 'All up to "H" fall out and go back to your depot', so Doug escaped his trip abroad.

Staff shortages in both world wars were made good by using 'the gentler sex' and in addition to working in offices, women fulfilled such duties as porters, ticket collectors, guards and engine cleaners, and some even worked on the permanent way.

One signalwoman's handbag caused delay on the single track line between Bristol and Radstock. With the Economic System of Permanent Way Mainten-ance, when a permanent way trolley was required to travel part way through a section, a key was taken from a signal box, this operation disconnecting all the instruments when a slide was withdrawn. Until that key was returned into a lineside box after the trolley had been removed from the track, the person in the signal box was unable to use the instruments. Unfortunately, this particular signalwoman had hung her bag on the slide; its weight pulled out the slide slightly and thus disconnected her instruments. She got into a panic and instituted pilot working to avoid any head-on collision. The repair lineman quickly spotted the source of the trouble.

During the Second World War some Bristol footplate men refused to work a lodging turn, where they would stay away overnight, and pressed to return to their home shed at the end of a duty. This was because it was not unknown for them to endure bombing at Bristol, then suffer another raid elsewhere during their lodging turn rest period, followed by yet another raid when they returned home.

Due to the delays caused by hectic traffic conditions, the drivers' wives could never be certain when their husbands would come home. Alone in the house, they were frightened in an air raid, yet if they knew their husbands were going to be absent arrangements could be made to stay with a friend or relative. In times of rationing, wives found catering difficult as they did not know when their husbands would be home for a meal. In order to resolve the situation, a meeting was called between ASLEF (the Associated Society of Locomotive Engineers and Firemen) and Colonel Harold Rudgard, the LMS Line Superintendent. The men suggested a solution: the three booked turns of lodging work per week be reduced to two; also, to ease the long hours on the road, relief points should be established between Bristol and Birmingham, and food should be provided to men on a lodging turn. These suggestions were adopted and relief points established at Ashchurch and Bromsgrove, while tins of sausages, sardines and soup were issued to men on lodging turns. One LMS Bath footplate man had left one Monday, worked his way to Carlisle and did not return to Bath until Thursday. With wartime rationing, finding food when you were away from home for four days was a concern until the railway issued supplies.

The war also brought unusual locomotives to the area. S160 class 2-8-0s were built in the USA for use by its invading army and between January 1943 and February 1944, 175 of these engines were temporarily allocated to the GWR. During 1944 I remember seeing trains of about five S160 locomotives coupled together being hauled through Bath en route from the arrival port to Swindon.

Between 1943 and 1945 Swindon built 80 class 8F 2-8-0s of LMS design and painted in LMS livery, albeit with GWR-style buffer beam numbers. The GWR used them until they were sent to the LMS after the war.

The Southern Railway had a surplus of engines due to the wartime reduction of its passenger service. Ten Drummond S11 class 4-4-0s and a T9 of the same wheel arrangement were used on the S&D and the LMS at Bath. Although sometimes used on S&D freight trains, their brakes were wholly inadequate for such working on a hilly route. Harry Whitaker, District Locomotive Superintendent, told Driver Fred Holmes, 'You can take 20 minerals [coal wagons].' 'Yes,' said Fred, 'if I have the brakes down on 19 of them.'

SR K10 class 4-4-0 No 137, on loan to Gloucester shed, appeared one day on the 10.30 pm Bath to Bristol goods train, consisting of about 30 wagons. Working round the tight curve and climbing the gradient of 1 in 100 between Mangotsfield South Junction and the station, it reached an accommodation crossing which enabled cattle to pass from a field on one side of the line to the other. Unfortunately, the cows did not always remember to wipe their hooves before going over, so consequently the crossing was plastered with mud and dung, causing No 137 to lose her feet. She slipped so severely that the driver closed the regulator. Unnoticed, the steam reversing gear fell into back gear so that when the driver re-opened the regulator, the train reversed. Quite unaware that he was going in the wrong direction because the blackout sheeting enclosed the cab, he was surprised to find his train derailed at the trap points protecting the South Junction.

Driver Bob Ford drove SR S11 class 4-4-0 No 404 with a full load of 210 tons out of Bath. He was impressed with her performance. She sat down on the rails and 'walked up the [1 in 50] bank as if there was nothing behind her'. She came out of the Midford end of Combe Down Tunnel with the safety valve blowing off. He was so impressed that he told the locomotive foreman that it was better than an LMS class 2P. No 404 was then tried on the 8.30 am Bath to Templecombe train, normally worked by a class 4F 0-6-0 because the load of six coaches, a parcels van and two milk tanks was 236–240 tons and certainly over the limit of 210 tons which could normally be handled by a 4-4-0 – yet No 404 was able to handle this load.

Although the LMS class 2P 4-4-0s were good engines, once in fog, a member of the class slipped to a stop on the S&D in Oldfield Park when the rails were covered in slime. Fireman Bob Ford climbed down from the footplate, took sand out of the boxes and sanded the rails for about 30 ft, additionally dropping fine chippings from the ballast. After this treatment, his driver successfully started the train.

Following D-day, many German prisoners-of-war were captured and travelled in Britain by rail. To help prevent prisoners escaping, signalmen were instructed to try to avoid stopping such trains, but in practice this was not always feasible.

Farleigh Down signal box and sidings just east of Bath, came into use in 1938 to deal with ammunition traffic stored in nearby stone quarries. It was a modern brick-built box with electric light and a kettle. During the war, the signalmen there worked twelve-hour shifts – quite a long time to be on your own. One signalman overcame this problem by drilling a hole in the floor to give access to the electric socket in the locking room and plugging in a radio. The aerial was no problem – he simply used a crocodile clip to attach the aerial to the telephone wires and got marvellous reception. Unfortunately, he was not the only one to get marvellous reception. The sound travelled along the wire to the District Control at Bristol and his crafty scheme was discovered. When this form of entertainment stopped, he dreamed up another. A keen fisherman, he made a 20-ft-long rod so that he could fish from his box.

The box was heated by a coal range. The allowance of 15 cwt of coal was insufficient for a box manned 24 hours a day, so ingenuity had to be brought into play to augment the supply. When the signalman knew that a light engine was coming, he unhitched the signal wire to render that signal inoperable. He then had to stop the light engine to give a written order to pass that signal at danger. The driver was invited to enter the box to have a cup of tea while the order was written out, the invitation being almost invariably accepted as there were no urgent wartime supplies being hauled.

While the driver was feeling under an obligation to the signalman, he would be asked if he would request his fireman to throw off some coal from the tender, sometimes as much as ten cwt being dropped. The engine then went on its way and the wire was reconnected.

12

TRAGEDY ON THE LINE

Thankfully **no major rail accident** has ever happened in the Bath/Bristol area, but there have been quite a number of serious incidents.

THE DOWN MAIL

On 6 June 1865 a double-headed Down express stopped east of Keynsham as one of the drivers had felt a thump and believed his engine might have been damaged. In those days time, rather than space, separated trains – they were held at Bath or Bristol for ten minutes after the previous train had left – so the guard was required by the rule book to walk back to protect the rear of his train. When recalled by the engine whistle he then planted a fusee, a device like a Roman candle firework which, when struck smartly, burned for ten minutes. Its light could be seen from a considerable distance and warned an approaching train that another had left that spot very recently.

The guard had returned to his train and it was just about to proceed when it was struck by the Down Mail. Three men in the end compartment of the last coach had a very fortunate escape. Its doors were locked according to regulations, but luckily one man possessed a carriage key and, seeing the approaching train, all were able to make their escape before the Mail engine struck. Approximately 15 passengers in other compartments were injured.

The Mail train guard, stupefied by the collision, was slow at protecting his train. He had only walked back about 150 yards when a Down empty carriage train passed him and struck the rear of the Mail. Both the Mail and the empty carriage train had been kept at Bath for the regulatory ten minutes, but as at that period there were no intermediate signals at night between Bath and Bristol, there were no means of maintaining this time interval.

The coach roofs of the period were fitted with outside luggage racks and one rather gruesome detail recorded by a contemporary newspaper was that, on arrival at Bristol, a dead Shetland pony was found lying on the roof of a first-class coach of the express, where it had been thrown by the force of the collision.

THE *FLYING DUTCHMAN*

A terrible tragedy was averted by a brave man on 31 March 1876. John Chiddy was foreman of Birchwood Quarry near the eastern mouth of Bristol No 2 Tunnel. A passing train had dislodged a large stone from a stack beside the line, which fouled the Down line. Realising that the fastest train in the world, the Down *Flying Dutchman*, was imminent, John struggled to shift the stone clear of the track. Just in time he succeeded, but the engine struck and killed him before he could leap clear. At that point the line ran on a ledge above the Avon and had the train been derailed, it would have plunged into the river with considerable loss of life.

The spot where the Flying Dutchman *would have plunged into the Avon had John Chiddy not saved it. The west portal of Bristol No 3 Tunnel can be seen, c.1850.* (J.C. Bourne)

How much did those thankful passengers contribute to a fund for John Chiddy's family? £3.17s 0d! It was a pathetic amount for a wife and seven children who had lost father and breadwinner. One person, Lord Elcho, hearing about the matter, was so incensed that he took up the case in Parliament. He asserted that if a man risked his life to save others, he should do so 'with the consciousness that his family would not be dependent on charity or the workhouse'. The Chancellor of the Exchequer explained that no funds were available to help such people. However, the press publicity resulted in one account being opened in Bath and another in Bristol. The Bank of England contributed £10 when informed that two of its officials were on that train with a large quantity of gold.

The total of £400 eventually subscribed purchased half an acre of land on which the six-bedroom Memorial Cottage was built, in what is now Memorial Road on the Hanham bank of the Avon. The smallholding brought in a sufficient income to pay Mrs Chiddy's day-to-day expenses. A plaque on the north side of the house carries the inscription: 'Erected AD 1877 by public subscription for the widow and family of John Chiddy who was killed by an express train whilst removing a large stone from the metals of the Great Western Railway near Conham, March 31st 1876.'

Just four months later, on 27 July 1876, the Up *Flying Dutchman* was headed by 4-2-4T No 2001 which had been built in Bristol eight years previously. Descending the gradient of 1 in 180 on the Bristol side of Flax Bourton Tunnel at about 65 mph, the engine's oscillation became violent, then it jumped off the track, crossed the Down line and struck the side of the cutting, causing No 2001 to fall over on its side. Fortunately, the coupling chain between the engine and coaches snapped, allowing the carriages to pass the engine and not pile up against it.

Guard John Watts in the leading van, despite a broken arm, sprained ankle and cuts, had the presence of mind to collect two red flags from his wrecked van and issue them to passengers to walk along the line on either side of the derailment in order to warn approaching trains, for debris had blocked both tracks.

Fireman James Randall had been killed instantly and Driver Dunscombe fatally injured, dying 20 minutes after the crash. Owing to the strength and stability of the broad gauge, the passengers escaped almost scot-free. Only the first coach was derailed, but a number of passengers slightly cut themselves when climbing out through the windows after having smashed them. This was necessary as the doors were locked on both sides. The 14 injured passengers were taken to Long Ashton where they were received hospitably by the villagers.

The Flax Bourton accident, 27 July 1876. A not-too-accurate drawing as the smoke box door is too small and the two cylinder covers are not precisely placed. The locomotive's number appears to be on the front of the tender, which being a tank engine, it did not have!
(Courtesy *Illustrated London News*)

One who was offered a derisory sum of one shilling as compensation had it raised to £450 by the Court.

And the cause of the accident? It was attributed to poor permanent way. The GWR had taken over the line from the B&E only six months previously. The latter had only carried out minimum maintenance before takeover and the GWR had failed to improve the line sufficiently quickly. No 2001 was so badly damaged that she was scrapped and the following year the other three engines of the class were converted to tender engines, as opinion then believed that tank engines were unsuited for express train haulage.

TAKING ITS TOLL

The toll footbridge across the Avon on the south side of the GWR station at Bath offered a convenient short cut to Lyncombe Hill when the 100th Bath & West Show was being held beside the Wells Road on a site now occupied by the Poets' Avenues.

To drum up patronage, the bridge proprietors erected near the station exit a sheet of canvas several feet in length which announced in large red and blue letters: 'The nearest way to the show field over this bridge. Toll one halfpenny.'

On 6 June 1877 a crowd of 200 to 300 from one train overwhelmed the toll keeper on the further bank and their weight caused the bridge to collapse with the loss of ten lives – nine killed outright and one dying later. More than 50 people were injured. The proprietors were successfully prosecuted for manslaughter.

Interestingly the replacement footbridge, still standing, was designed by T.E.M. Marsh, formerly resident engineer at Bath for the Bath to Bristol section of the GWR.

LANDSLIDE

On 27 February 1900, after excessive rain, 3,000 tons of earth and stone slipped in the cutting east of Saltford Tunnel, covering the Down line for 40 yards. Then, before it could be warned, the 4.40 pm from Salisbury plunged into the landslide, derailing the engine and the first four coaches, throwing them over to the Up line. It was fortunate that the train was running late, so had passed the Up train before reaching the slip, otherwise the Up train would have crashed into the Down.

As the cutting had such a steep slope, working to clear the obstruction was fraught with difficulties. A hundred men had ropes tied round their waists, with the other ends secured to strong stakes driven into the field above. When darkness fell, they worked by the light of naphtha flares. Twice the wagons being filled with the debris were buried by further slides, and the stout chains used in an attempt to draw the wagons clear snapped under the strain of the locomotives pulling them.

The Up line was opened on the following noon. In order to facilitate single-line working pending the opening of the Down line, an electric single-line staff system was introduced between Saltford and Keynsham. A temporary facing crossover was laid at Saltford, worked from a ground frame, its two levers locked by an Annett's key from Saltford signal box.

TERROR IN THE TUNNEL

Perhaps the most dramatic accident in the area happened on the S&D on 20 November 1929 after S&D class 7F 2-8-0 No 89 left Evercreech Junction with 32 wagons each loaded with coal, a loaded goods wagon, three empty wagons, an empty oil tank and a 20-ton brake van. Due to poor steaming on the climb to Combe Down Tunnel, No 89 entered at only 4 mph. Fortunately the engine was travelling tender-first, so the fumes from the chimney were behind the cab.

Nevertheless the single bore tunnel, over a mile in length and without any ventilating shafts, was exceedingly hot and smoky. Fireman Pearce was forced by choking fumes to wrap a coat round his head and sit down, after which he remembered nothing, gases rendering him unconscious. In due course, Driver Jennings too followed him into oblivion.

Now completely unattended, No 89 continued to plod up the gradient of 1 in 100 through the tunnel. At the other end was the 1 in 50 descent to Bath. No 89, with the gradient and the weight of 38 vehicles behind her, picked up speed. Guard Christopher Wagner applied the handbrake in his van, but without the help of the locomotive and tender brakes, it was really only a gesture.

S&D class 7F 2-8-0 No 89 overturned at Bath after running away, 20 November 1929. A flagman, right, controls trains past the disaster. (Author's collection)

At an estimated speed of 50 to 60 mph No 89 derailed at the entrance to Bath goods yard, overturning and its wagons piling up against her. A live coal from No 89 was flung through an open bedroom window in Albert Buildings where it caught the house alight, but was soon put out. The goods cabin was destroyed, killing Inspector John Norman. A clerk taking a short cut through the yard was also killed. Driver Jennings died on his way to the Royal United Hospital and Fireman Pearce was severely injured. Guard Wagner, anticipating a derailment, jumped from his van and received compound fractures to both legs. Ironically, had he remained in it he would have been unharmed, for after the crash it still remained upright with his hand lamp burning brightly.

When newspaper photographers arrived from London to take pictures of the disaster, the LMS denied them permits. Using their wits, they boarded a Bath to Bristol passenger train which fortunately for them drew to a standstill close by the accident and thus were able to take the desired pictures.

At the inquiry the general consensus of opinion from S&D drivers was that if the tunnel was entered from the Midford end at a fair speed, they were not in it sufficiently long for conditions to become serious; trouble only arose if they had to stop at Midford and then restart with a heavy load.

Colonel A.C. Trench wrote in his report to the Ministry of Transport that it was the first instance in over 50 years that an engine crew had been overcome by fumes and 'under normal conditions the atmospheric conditions are not such as to involve any risk of anything more than a degree of discomfort'. He said that providing a ventilating shaft or fan would be too expensive, but a practical remedy would be a reduction of the load of an Up train.

The railway decided to change to providing Welsh coal at Bath, rather than North coal as hitherto. This was because Welsh coal did not produce so many fumes, though even with Welsh coal, footplate men often dipped a wiper (cloth) into a bucket of cold water and placed it over their face and, if necessary, knelt on the floor where they found cooler and fresher air. Emerging from even the relatively short 447-yard-long Devonshire Tunnel, an engine would be saturated with water, with yellow sulphur drying on it.

Normally going towards Bath, an S&D engine would be 'disposed of' on its arrival, so knowing this, the fire was generally levelled when approaching Radstock and no more coal would be added. If sometimes a fireman felt a little more was needed before reaching Combe Down Tunnel, he fired as soon after Midford as possible in order to avoid making smoke in the tunnel. In the other direction, going through the tunnel was downhill, so firing was unnecessary.

And what happened to No 89? She was repaired, put back in service, continuing to work over the S&D until withdrawal in June 1964. She was eventually saved for preservation.

The tunnel was never a place to linger. One day a class 3F 0-6-0 was working to Bath with Locomotive Inspector Wickson on the footplate. He always wore a stiff white collar. The class 3F lost her feet in Combe Down Tunnel and slipped to a standstill. Eventually they reversed out to the Midford end, as the only alternative was remaining in the tunnel and suffocating. Due to the fact that he had been perspiring with the heat, frustration and fear of what would happen to him, Wickson's stiff white collar was like a wet rag.

A Comedy of errors

On 29 July 1936 a comedy of errors took place on the S&D. Driver Rawlings and Fireman Parker were on the footplate of class 3F 0-6-0T No 7620 shunting at Writhlington Colliery Sidings on the Bath side of Radstock. They were standing with a rake of wagons on the Up main line when Driver Rawlings espied class 7F 2-8-0 No 13803 approaching on the same line, running away and having come through the protecting signals.

Rawlings observed that its footplate was empty as its crew had jumped off and were busily applying the wagon brakes as the train passed them. Rawlings, quickly seeking a way to avoid the collision, opened his regulator, slowly at first, so as not to bump the wagons in front of him and thus cause a derailment, but when they were all completely buffered up, he opened the regulator fully.

Seeing himself as a hero going to the rescue, he jumped off No 7620 and on to the footplate of No 13803, where he fully closed the regulator and brought the runaway to a halt within three engine lengths. Unfortunately his fireman failed to hear his shout to remain on the engine and, believing his driver was bailing out, jumped off on the opposite side. So now the situation had No 13803 brought to a halt and No 7620 running away propelling eight wagons before it.

When Fireman Parker realised that he had been intended to remain on No 7620 he chased after it, but lost the race. No 7620 roared through Wellow at a speed which the signalman estimated at 50 mph and continued to Midford. Here the track became single and at the points, seven of the wagons derailed, skittling down signals, telegraph poles and Signalman Larcombe's box, though fortunately not harming him. The stationmaster, hearing a loud crash, threw himself on the floor of his office as debris spread over a distance of 140 yards. The railway here was on the ledge of a hillside and six wagons fell 40 ft into a garden, the owner of which obtained the wreckage for firewood at a very reasonable figure.

Signalman Larcombe at Midford showed great presence of mind. The railway telegraph wires had been wrecked by the derailment and so were useless. He ran to a nearby house to use the GPO telephone and thus warn Bath Control of the events. The office in turn made arrangements with the Bath Junction signal box to direct the runaway into the goods yard and staff in the Bath Locomotive office were ordered to leave immediately as it would pass only inches from the office wall.

In the event the emergency plan was not needed. No 7620 kept going, pushing in front of her, like a coster's barrow, the remains of a wagon running on only two wheels. Remarkably the engine and half a wagon succeeded in negotiating the mile-long Combe Down Tunnel, but at Claude Avenue Bridge, about halfway between the north portal of Devonshire Tunnel and Bath Junction, the end door of the wagon fell off, derailing the No 7620 and bringing her to a halt. About the same time, owing to a shortage of water, the fusible plug on the firebox crown melted and the fire was put out by water from the boiler pouring into the firebox. No 7620's solo journey was over.

Class 3F 0-6-0T, No 7620 at Bath Junction, being drawn from Claude Avenue Bridge, (where it came to a halt), to Bath locomotive depot, following its runaway from Writhlington 29 July 1936. A notice in the foreground advertises Cleveland petrol at 1s 4d a gallon. (Author's collection)

13

THE GLORIES OF THE PAST

One man who remembers well the age of steam in Bristol and Bath is Colin Roberts. 'These days,' he says, 'I do a lot of research and find it very interesting looking back at the glories of the past.' From locomotive spotter, to British Railways clerk, to railway researcher – Colin has seen the railways from every perspective.

'It all started at Staple Hill, the local station where, at a very young age, I was taken by family members to watch trains. Then in the mid-1930s, on at least one occasion we made a journey to Bristol St Philip's station situated at the top end of Old Market, close to a busy shopping area. On returning to the station and looking at our engine before boarding the train for our homeward run, I was invited on the footplate and shown the fire! I can recollect it having an enclosed cab, so it must have been one of the Johnson 0-4-4Ts so numerous on the LMS at that time.

My first spotting took place on Friday afternoons in the summer of 1941 when I was nine years old. Along with a neighbour and her daughter, my mother took my young sister Valerie and me to Rodway Hill for a picnic. Here was a wonderful view of Mangotsfield station and the line to Bristol. Local trains to Gloucester could be seen, together with those to Bath via Bitton, with a few expresses serving Birmingham and the north. In 1942 my cousin Graham, a few years older than myself, joined us on these expeditions. The seeds sown, this initiation ultimately led to railway employment for both of us.

An interesting sighting was the evening freight train from St Philip's to Bath often drawn by a Southern Railway K10 class 4-4-0 on loan to the LMS during the Second World War. Of particular interest was the Down express which was usually loaded to twelve coaches and pulled by a Jubilee class 4-6-0. Due to the length of the train, after the initial stop, it had to draw forward to let passengers in the rear portion disembark and allow any parcels to be unloaded from the guard's compartment. Engines seen included No 5657 *Tyrwhitt*, No 5679 *Armada* and No 5696 *Arethusa*. On one occasion we went via a subway to the station and awaited its arrival. To my great delight the engine came to a stop opposite me – it was No 5724 *Warspite*.

By 1943 I was allowed to visit Staple Hill station – the nearest to my home – by myself. The first Ian Allan ABCs were now available showing all locomotives owned by the respective railway companies. Purchasing an *ABC of LMS Locomotives* added more interest to the hobby and a similar *ABC of GWR Locomotives* was soon bought. The nearest places where I could observe Great Western engines were Stapleton Road, Lawrence Hill, or Bristol Temple Meads. I now knew what class a locomotive belonged to and to which depot it was allocated by observing the smoke box-sited shed plate of LMS engines, or on GWR engines, by the stencilled abbreviation of the place-name at the front end frame behind the buffer beam.

My hobby was partly restricted because, during the war years, photography of trains or railway installations was not allowed, neither were shed visits permitted. This was because there was a possibility of spies trying to infiltrate and disrupt the railway network.

The smallest locomotive I ever saw running through Staple Hill under its own power was ex-Lancashire & Yorkshire Railway "Pug" 0-4-0ST No 11202 toddling back to Radstock from Barrow Road shed, Bristol. It was possibly in December 1943 after a light service repair. Running on its own was very unusual because its light weight could not be relied upon to activate the track circuit equipment. A signalman, therefore, would not know if an engine had passed a certain point which was out of his sight.

At Staple Hill on 18 March 1944 I first saw a rare sight – Jubilee No 5682 *Trafalgar* on an express for Bristol. It was a London engine allocated to 14B, Kentish Town. Another interesting engine was No 5719 *Glorious* from 26A Newton Heath, Manchester which appeared on 28 March 1944. On another day I saw No 5670 *Howard of Effingham* from 12B Carlisle Upperby shed and No 5715 *Invincible* from 12A Carlisle Kingmoor, both far from home on unrecorded dates in 1944.

One Sunday evening during April 1944, after Jubilee class 4-6-0 No 5654 *Hood* had passed with the Up Mail, a surprise was in store for me. Ex-Lancashire & Yorkshire Railway 0-8-0 No 12831 appeared with an 18D Staveley shed plate, running a light engine to Barrow Road after bringing a freight to Westerleigh Sidings.

I also visited Fishponds station, situated at the top of the steep incline from Barrow Road. I well remember one occasion when a rare engine in these parts, Jubilee No 5623 *Palestine* of 8A, Edge Hill, Liverpool shed, breasted the incline with the wartime equivalent of the northbound Devonian.

Sometimes when visiting my grandmother at Greenbank, after getting off the bus at Royate Hill, I made a detour via Clay Bottom where Kingswood Junction signal box was located. There on one occasion I grew very excited when I saw on the line to Bristol an ambulance train hauled by LNER class B12 No 8518, while another time Messrs Peckett & Sons Ltd works locomotive 0-6-0ST *Nancy* was at the exchange sidings with a wagon.

Around 1945 I invested my pocket money in Saturday afternoon trips to Temple Meads with my cousin Graham. We travelled to Stapleton Road station by bus and then bought a 2½d return ticket for rail travel to Temple Meads. In due course we returned to Stapleton Road by the Avonmouth service hauled by a Dean Goods 0-6-0 which was always rostered for this train.

On arrival we would quickly cross over to the South Wales platform and watch Star class 4-6-0 No 4031 *Queen Mary* of Stafford Road, Wolverhampton, shed, with the Penzance to Wolverhampton express, gaining what speed she could, as no stop would be made here for banking assistance up the incline to Filton. Several years later the service was named "The Cornishman".

There were some visits to Stapleton Road station after school, which allowed me to see the 10.10 am Penzance to Manchester express via the Severn Tunnel go through with Bulldog 4-4-0 No 3406 *Calcutta*, or No 3453 *Seagull*, both of Pontypool Road shed, piloting a Bristol Bath Road Castle class 4-6-0.

A visit to Barrow Road on 25 March 1946 found Kirtley double-framed class 2F 0-6-0 No 22630, built in November 1870 and shedded at 21B Bournville, having just received a Heavy Service repair in the Bristol works. Along with a few others of the class it had been kept for working the branch from Halesowen to Longbridge where heavier locomotives were not permitted.

Stanier class 8F 2-8-0s were infrequent visitors to Bristol at that time, consequently Midland class 3F 0-6-0s were still arriving from distant sheds – for example, No 3446 from 20C Royston, near Leeds.

Early in 1948, following railway nationalisation, a new system of numbering of locomotive stock was introduced to avoid confusion between those locomotives from various companies which carried the same number. This system superseded a regional prefix letter which had many disadvantages. Ex-GWR engines retained their original number, but at the front, instead of the number being painted on the buffer beam, it was placed on a smoke box number plate. There were numerous times when the smoke box number plate had not yet been cast and the locomotive went back into traffic without it.

Some evenings I went to Staple Hill to see what was on the northbound Mail and the Down Newcastle. It was early May 1949 when I met a friend who was just returning from visiting Barrow Road shed, who told me that the foreman there had shown him a letter stating that next week they would have a 1B Camden London Jubilee class No 45741 *Leinster* on loan for a week. It sounded too good to be true, but sure enough, she was actually here working from Bristol. Seeing was believing on Thursday, 12 May 1949.

There was a small repair works at Barrow Road which could take up to three engines. On Sunday, 12 June 1949 it contained class 3F 0-6-0T "Jinties" No 7496 of 22C Bath and No 7678, 22A Bristol, along with ex-Midland class 2F 0-6-0 No 3062 also of Bristol. Just having left the works after attention, Midland class 2P No 364 of 17B Burton-on-Trent shed was in the yard. There were also visiting Midland and LMS Compound class 4P 4-4-0s No 41037 of 19B Millhouses, Sheffield and No 41047 from 21A Saltley, Birmingham. In evidence were Midland class 3P 4-4-0s No 40741 of Bristol and No 40743 from Saltley. I was fortunate to see them as locomotives of this class were fast disappearing. On shed, possibly awaiting attention in the works, was Midland class 1P 0-4-4T No 1322 from 22E Highbridge. Engines of this latter class, a design dating from 1881, were only a few years previously still working the Bristol to Bath service.

On 2 January 1950 I entered British Railways service as a clerk in the Midland Road Goods Department, then situated in the Midland Region but which passed to the Western Region that April. Other types of employment had not suited me. My heart was in the railway: the salary was less, but I was now happy.

It had not been an easy entry, the demanding examination involving general knowledge, a wide acquaintance with the geography of Great Britain, especially in the area formerly served by the LMS, and an arithmetic test. After successfully passing these hurdles, I was sent to be medically examined by the London Midland Region doctor at Bath.

The offices at Midland Road were gas-lit and heated with coal fires. Telephones were of the old type where the mouthpiece was on top of an upright stem and the earpiece on the end of the flex. The GPO telephone directory was protected by a cover that had originally graced a London, Tilbury & Southend Railway timetable. The desks were high and in rows, seating was on high stools. Now I was able to see at first-hand how the railway worked. I was no longer just a spotter.

Locomotive spotting was a very popular activity in the 1950s and 60s. Enthusiasts at Temple Meads note class 5 4-6-0 No 45265 and 43XX class 2-6-0 No 6399, 14 June 1958. (R.E. Toop)

My job consisted of preparing delivery sheets to be checked against goods arriving in various wagons. These sheets were prepared from invoices received from sending stations. Some invoices travelled in an envelope under the label on the side of a wagon, while others came by passenger train in order to arrive before the consignment to which they referred.

Invoices and letters were carried economically by the railway to avoid payment to the Post Office. The railway had a very efficient internal letter sorting and delivery system to its various departments. Each area was allocated a letter sorting office number: Bristol was 55. Letters were placed in a foolscap envelope with nine squares on the front where the number of the delivery area was written. The flap was tucked in and not sealed, in order that the envelope could be re-used; re-cycling is nothing new. Between the main rail centres, mail was carried in large leather satchels. At the local sorting office, arriving letters were sorted and given to various train guards to deliver to the stations.

The road transport consisted of 3- and 6-ton Scammell mechanical horses and 1- and 3-ton Dennis's, some of which were flat-bed lorries, while others had sides, hoops and tarpaulin cover which could be converted to a van. There were additionally a few 5-ton Vulcan lorries and a host of horse drays for town delivery work. These vehicles all had the name of the secretary, followed by 'Euston Station'. There was one with larger diameter rear wheels for passenger train parcels delivery inscribed 'Waterloo Station' – possibly it had come off the Somerset and Dorset line. Goods vehicles generally delivered to shops and commercial premises in the morning and collected in the afternoon.

Adjacent to the goods offices was St Philip's passenger station, very much in its final years, but I was able to travel to it from my local station at Staple Hill. I travelled home to lunch using a convenient service which terminated at Mangotsfield. There were some friendly drivers who allowed me footplate trips. Usually the train was headed by a Stanier class 3P 2-6-2T, one of them, No 40116 had just come from 14B, Kentish Town, London and the cab was in a very dirty condition. On one occasion the train was worked by an Ivatt class 4MT 2-6-0.

March 1950 saw the arrival at Bristol of 2-6-6-2T Beyer-Garratts from Toton after working through to Westerleigh Sidings on an evening mineral train. The return was the following morning. My first observation was on 12 March when No 47970 had been stopped for repair to a valve spindle guide.

I had a few spells at Fishponds station when relief was required. The goods office there was just inside the yard gates, only a short distance from the main line where heavier trains would be toiling up the bank, nearing the end of the climb from Barrow Road. At this point the track was on a slight curve and as the Midland 4-4-0s went by on the local to Gloucester, I could hear clearly the ringing coupling rods.

An infrequent occurrence by then was the sight of a new locomotive from Messrs Peckett's Atlas Works brought up by the local shunt engine and taken to Westerleigh for onwards working to its destination in the Midlands.

Another locomotive type at Barrow Road I never expected to see was Great Western King class No 6017 *King Edward IV*. On 8 October 1950 it was outside at the back of the main shed, adjacent to the works awaiting attention, possibly to a hot axle box. Although the repair shops at Bath Road were capable of carrying out the work required, they lacked a wheel-drop. Sending it to the King to Barrow Road repair

Colin Roberts

shops avoided the troublesome high lift of a heavy locomotive because there the engine could simply stand over a pit and the appropriate set of wheels dropped.

In February 1951 I was sent to Yate as relief clerk in the goods department for a few days, soon being transferred permanently, and stayed 16 years – but that is another story.

In the latter days of steam I visited Barrow Road shed and by then an interesting mix of all four main line companies' engines could be seen, together with British Railways' Standard locomotives. The Southern Region engines would all have been withdrawn from service and on their way to a South Wales scrapyard.

Today, although I am interested in the modern railway, my memories of those earlier times are wonderful to recall, and most of my notes survive. There were a few occasions in the latter days of steam when I was making notes and saying to myself, "I wonder if I will ever look at this again?" It was a grand life on the railway – I thoroughly enjoyed it!'

14

STEAM TODAY

When the S&D and the Bristol-Mangotsfield-Bath line closed to passenger traffic on 6 March 1966, it seemed that steam in the Bristol/Bath area had gone for good. But this was not the case.

In 1972 the Bristol Suburban Railway Society was given permission to use Bitton station as a base from which it was hoped that a line could be reopened to Bristol and Bath and a commuter service operated. Two years later trains were running on 100 yards of track which on 6 March 1991 extended to Oldland Common. As the original aim of restoring a commuter line was seen to be over-ambitious, it was renamed the Avon Valley Railway. The line has been extended eastwards from Bitton to a station at Avonside Riverside where a landing stage and picnic area were established. There are high hopes that the line will be extended yet again to Kelston and then Newbridge on the outskirts of Bath.

In Bristol, the Bristol Harbour Railway runs along part of the southern bank of the Floating Harbour between Prince Street Bridge and the SS *Great Britain*. It offers the experience of an industrial, rather than main line, or branch, railway.

In addition to these two preserved lines, steam specials operate quite frequently from London to Bristol/Bath, and rather less often from Bristol westwards.

Edwin Hulse, *a Bristol-built Avonside locomotive at the Avon Valley Railway, Bitton, 8 May 1976.* (Author)

Bibliography

Channon, G., *Bristol & the Promotion of the Great Western Railway*, Bristol, Historical Association, 1985

Clinker, C.R., *Register of Closed Passenger Stations & Goods Depots*, Weston-super-Mare, Avon-Anglia, 1988

Coleman, T., *The Railway Navvies*, Harmondsworth, Penguin, 1968

Cooke, R.A., *Track Layout Diagrams of the GWR & BR WR*, Section 19A, 19B, 20 & Section 21, Harwell, Author, 1992, 1996, 1988, 1987

Leitch, R., *The Railways of Keynsham*, Long Stratton, Railway Correspondence & Travel Society, 1977

Lyons, E., *An Historical Survey of Great Western Engine Sheds 1947*, Oxford, OPC, 1974

Lyons, E. & Mountford, E., *An Historical Survey of Great Western Sheds 1837–1947*, Oxford, 1979

MacDermot, E.T., Clinker, C.R. & Nock, O.S., *History of the Great Western Railway*, London, Ian Allan, 1964 and 1967

Maggs, C.G., *Bristol Railway Panorama*, Bath, Millstream, 1990

Maggs, C.G., *Rail Centres: Bristol*, London, Ian Allan, 1996

Maggs, C.G., *The GWR Bristol to Bath Line*, Stroud, Sutton Publishing, 2001

Maggs, C.G., *The GWR Swindon to Bath Line*, Stroud, Sutton Publishing, 2003

Maggs, C.G., *The Mangotsfield to Bath Line*, Usk, Oakwood Press, 2005

Maggs, C.G., *The Bristol Port Railway & Pier*, Usk, Oakwood Press, 1975

Maggs, C.G., *Somerset & Dorset: Life on the Bath to Bournemouth Line*, Hersham, Ian Allan, 2007

Maggs, C.G., *The Bristol & Gloucester Railway and the Avon & Gloucestershire Railway*, Headington, Oakwood Press, 1992

Norris, J., *The Bristol & South Wales Union Railway*, London, Railway & Canal Historical Society, 1985

Vincent, M., *Lines to Avonmouth*, Oxford, OPC, 1979

Vincent, M., *Reflections on the Portishead Branch*, Oxford, OPC, 1983

Appendix

Bristol and Bath Railway Chronology

	Opened	Closed
Combe Down – Bath	1731	c.1760
Midford – Radstock	c.1814	c.1872
Coalpit Heath – Bitton	July 1832	09.07.1906
Bristol – Mangotsfield	06.08.1835	03.01.1970
Bristol – Bath	31.08.1840	
Chippenham to Bath	30.06.1841	
Bristol – Exeter	01.05.1844	
Bristol – Gloucester	06.07.1844	03.01.1970 (Bristol–Mangotsfield)
Hotwells – Avonmouth	06.03.1865	03.07.1922 (Hotwells–Sneyd Park Jnc)
Bristol - New Passage	08.09.1863	01.12 1886 (New Passage Pier)
Bristol – Portishead	18.04.1867	07.09.1964 (Passenger)
Mangotsfield – Bath	04.08 1869	28 05 1971
Bristol Harbour Railway	11.03.1872	11.01.1964
Bristol – Radstock	03.09.1873	14.07.1968
Evercreech Jnc – Bath	20.07.1874	07.03.1966
Clifton Extension Railway	24.02.1877	
Canon's Marsh Branch	04.10.1906	14.06.1965

Index

Aird, John 23
Albright & Wilson 69
Allen, Ralph 6
Ashman, William 6
Ashton 24
Atlas Engineering Works 58f, 121
Avon 5, 27, 40, 96
Avon & Gloucestershire Railway 6f
Avon Valley Railway 68, 122f
Avonmouth 18f, 21, 23, 50, 54, 58, 67ff, 75, 92ff, 97, 99
Avonside Engine Co 57, 61, 122
Avonside Wharf 10, 71

Baillie, W. 26
Bath 5, 8f, 11f, 13ff, 27ff, 40f, 69, 73f, 85, 99ff, 109
Bath & Cheltenham Gazette 35
Bath & Twerton Co-operative Society 74f
Bath & West Agricultural Show 85
Bath Chronicle 35
Bath Tramways 86
Bathford 16
Bathurst Basin 24
Beaumont, Major 19
Bedminster 23
Bentley's 91
BGR 6, 8f
BHR 23ff, 123
Bingham, J. 26
Bitton 27f, 73, 84, 98

BNSR 26
Bond & Winwood 8
Bourne, J.C. 12, 66, 91, 106
BPRP 18f, 21, 54, 93
Bradshaw 91
bridge 10f, 14ff, 24ff, 27ff
Bristol 5f, 9f, 12f, 57, 92, 101
B&E 9, 11, 14, 57ff, 66, 77f, 89, 108
Bristol East Depot 74
Bristol & Gloucester Railway 8ff, 45, 70f
Bristol & Portishead Pier & Railway 23
Bristol Commercial Vehicles Ltd 26
Bristol Tramways & Carriage Co Ltd 61, 93f
Bristol Wagon & Carriage Works Co Ltd 61
Bristol West Depot 74
Bristol Suburban Railway Society 123
Brunel, I.K. 8, 10, 57, 77f
Brotherhood, Peter 23
Brotherhood, Rowland. 23
BSWUR 22f
Buckle, George E. 14
Bullard, Henry 55

Cammell, Laird & Co 61
Cam Valley 5

Canon's Marsh 24, 64, 69, 100
Cardiff 22f,
Carson's chocolate factory 72f
Cheltenham & Great Western Union Railway 8
Chiddy, John 106f
Chidgey Joseph C. 77
Chivers & Co 70
Church, St Mary's Redcliffe 71f
Clandown 6
Clifton College 18
CER 19ff, 46, 77
coal 39f, 46, 62, 111
Coalpit Heath 6, 70
Commonwealth Smelting Co Ltd 67
Crown Brickyard 67
Culverhouse, P.E. 78

Davey & Co Ltd 69
Daily Telegraph 90
Day, Dr 51, 97
Dunscombe, Mr 107

East Bristol Colliery 70
Edwards, John 13

Fairlie, Robert 57
Farleigh Down 103f
Festiniog Railway 57
Fishponds 58, 74
Flax Bourton 108
Ford, Bob 95f, 103
Fowler, John 61
Fox Francis 58, 78
Fox Francis W. 58
Fox, Walker & Co 58

Fox's Wood 40f
Francis, Frederick 56
Fry, Albert 61
Fry's chocolate factory
    64, 68f
Fry, Theodore 61

Grace, W.G. 27
Graphic 90
GWR 8ff, 16f, 21, 24,
    26f, 33, 39, 43f, 50f,
    54, 57, 61, 66, 69f,
    77f, 80, 86, 90, 92,
    95, 102, 108, 115
Gruning, Henry 57

Handyside, Henry 58
Hardy, Wyndham 9
Helen, Princess 80
Hill, Messrs 74
Holden, Doug 101
Holmes, Fred 37, 103
Hotwells 18, 20, 22

ICI 67
Illustrated London News
    90
Imperial Smelting Co
    Ltd 70

Jennings, Mr 110f
Jobbins, Charles 73
Jonathan, John 16

Keefe, J. 46
Kennet & Avon Canal
    5, 9, 74
Kelson, James 83
Kelston 54, 86
Keynsham 6, 42, 68f,
    105
King, Tommy 34
King's Wharf 71f
Knight, John 54

Larcombe, Mr 113
Lawrence Hill 61
Lean, W. 30
Leeds Forge Co Ltd 61
LMS 33, 45f, 51, 54,
    115
locomotives 8, 18, 21,
    33ff, 57ff
locomotive sheds:
    Bath GWR 48ff, 98
        101
    Bath MR 37, 39, 41,
        46ff, 117
    Bristol Barrow Road
        45f, 115ff
    Bristol Bath Road 34,
        40, 42f, 49, 58f,
        116, 121
    Bristol St Philip's
        Marsh 40, 43f
    Bristol South Wales
        Junction 35, 45
    Shirehampton 46
Longman's 91
Lowe, Joseph 56
Lysaght, John 65, 67,
    70

Mackay, Mr 16
Mangotsfield 6, 47, 54,
    71, 73, 103, 122
Marsh, T.E.M. 109
Marshall, H.B. 89
Marshall, William 89
May, Messrs 74
Measom, George 91
Midford 5, 30, 99, 112
MR 10, 18, 21, 27f, 39,
    50, 58, 61, 70f, 73f,
    78, 81, 86
Miller, Mr 46
mishaps 8, 12f, 14, 16,
    28, 30, 35, 54ff, 73,
    82, 85, 96, 103, 105ff

Monkton Combe School
    87
Murray's 91
Murray, Ronald 58

Nelson, John 9
New Passage Pier 22f
Newbridge 29, 123
Newport 23
Norman, John 111

oil gas 54
Orton, W. 77

Parker, Mr 112
Patchway 23
Pearce Mr 110
Peckett, Thomas 58f,
    68, 70f, 116, 121
Pines Express 54, 70
PBA 67ff, 92, 99
Portishead 18, 23, 69,
    92
Portskewett 23
Pylle Hill 15, 66

Radstock 5f, 26, 30,
    101,115
Randall, James 107
Rawlings, Mr 112
Ray, Rev. W.E 29
Railcar, diesel 44
Redcliffe, St Mary's 71,
    72
Reed Crane & Hoist Co
    Ltd 58
Richardson, Charles 23f
Roberts, Colin 114ff
Routledge 91
Rowe Brothers 64
Rudgard, Col 37, 102

Saltford 12, 28, 86f,
    109

Severn Tunnel 23, 44, 116
Shipp, Bert 37
Smith Mr 33
Shepton Mallet 56
Smith W.H 82, 90
Simms & Macintyre 91
Slaughter, Edward 57
Sneyd Park Junction 19f
S&D 29f, 46ff, 57, 74, 83, 989f, 103
Somerset Coal Canal 5, 26, 30
Stoke Gifford 75
South Wales Junction 23
South West Gas Board 69
Staddon, Frank 32
stations
    Ashton Gate 88
    Avon Riverside 123
    Bath GWR 11, 14, 27, 55, 80f, 96f
    Bath MR 28, 48 56, 73, 81f, 86, 90
    Bitton 73, 84, 122
    Brislington 26
    Bristol St Philip's 35ff, 70f, 73, 114, 120
    Bristol Temple Meads 10, 27, 51ff, 64, 66f, 70, 77ff, 97, 115f, 118
    Bristol Parkway 75, 79
    Chittening 93
    Clifton Bridge 23
    Clifton Down 20, 69, 79, 88, 93,

Fishponds 116, 120
Hallen 92
Henbury 93
Hotwells 20, 22, 93
Kelston 86, 98, 123
Keynsham 91
Lawrence Hill 115
Mangotsfield 71, 103, 114, 120
Nightingale Valley 23
Oldland Common 123
Parson Street 100
Portbury Shipyard 94
Redland 77
St Andrew's Road 93
St Anne's Park 41
Saltford 86, 97
Sea Mills 21
Shirehampton 92
Staple Hill 114f, 117, 120
Stapleton Road 69, 115f
Stoke Gifford 75
Stanley Engineering Co 69
Straker 74
Stothert, Henry A. 57
Stothert, George 57
Stothert & Pitt 69, 74
Square Grip Reinforcement Co 69
Sydney Gardens 80

Tate & Lyle 69
Thick ,W. 77
Times, The 14, 17, 90f
Trench, Col A.C. 111
Trollope, Anthony 91

tunnels
    Box 16
    Bristol 12f, 41, 97, 106
    Clifton Down 19ff
    Combe Down 30f, 56, 103, 110ff, 113
    Devonshire 30, 48, 85, 111
    Flax Bourton 107
    Saltford 12, 109
    Staple Hill 8
    Twerton 12ff, 97
    Willsbridge 7
turntable 37, 43, 46f
troughs, water 40ff

Victoria Bridge Road 41

Wagner, Christopher 110f
Walker, T. & C. 30f
Walker, Edwin 57f
Walkey & Son 89
Warmley 72
Watts, John 107
Weston 73
Weston-super-Mare 43, 88
Westerleigh sidings 70f, 74, 115, 120f
Weston, Clevedon & Portishead Light Railway 92
Whitaker, Harry 103
Wickson, Mr 112
Wiltshire Times 74
Writhlington 112
Wyatt, Sir M.D. 78
Yatton 55